Dialectical Social Theory and Its Critics

SUNY Series in Radical Social and Political Theory
Roger S. Gottlieb, Editor

Dialectical Social Theory and Its Critics

From Hegel to Analytical Marxism and Postmodernism

Tony Smith

State University of New York Press

Published by
State University of New York Press, Albany

Printed in the United States of America

For information, address State University of New York Press, State University Plaza, Albany, N.Y., 12246

Production by Marilyn P. Semerad
Marketing by Bernadette LaManna

Library of Congress Cataloging-in-Publication Data

Smith, Tony, 1951-
Dialectical social theory and its critics: from Hegel to analytical marxism and postmodernism / Tony Smith.
p. cm.—(SUNY series in radical social and political theory)
Includes bibliographical references and index.
ISBN 0-7914-1047-1.—ISBN 0-7914-1048-X (pbk.)
1. Marxian school of sociology. 2. Hegel, Georg Wilhelm Friedrich, 1770-1831—Contributions in dialectic. 3. Marx, Karl, 1818-1883—Contributions in dialectic. 4. Dialectic. 5. Marxian economics. 6. Postmodernism—Social aspects. I. Title. II. Series.
HM24.S5394 1992
301'.01—dc20 91-28605
CIP

10 9 8 7 6 5 4 3 2 1

Contents

Acknowledgments

An earlier version of Chapter I appeared in *Radical Philosophy* (no. 48, 1988, 30-35). Chapter III first appeared in *International Philosophical Quarterly* (30, no. 3, 190, 289-98). Sections of Chapter IV were published in *Owl of Minerva* (21, no. 1, 1989, 103-14). Earlier versions of Chapters V and VII can be found in their present titles in *Science and Society* (50, no. 2, 1986, 148-76; and 53, no. 3, 1989, 327-40, respectively). Chapter VI first appeared as the article "Analytical Marxism and Marx's systematic dialectical theory" in *Man and World* (23, 1990, 321-43), © 1990 Kluwer Academic Publishers, reprinted by permission of Kluwer Academic Publishers. A shorter version of Chapter VIII has been published by *Rethinking Marxism*. I would like to thank the editors of these journals for permission to use this material here. I would also like to thank Chris Arthur, James Dickinson, Fred Evans, Milton Fisk, Steven Gold, William McBride, and Joseph McCarney for the friendship and intellectual support they have provided during the writing of this book. The book is dedicated to Rebecca Burke.

Introduction

The nature of dialectics is among the most contentious issues in Marxist philosophy. In *Capital* and other writings Marx was clearly influenced by Hegel's dialectical theory. But in what exactly does this Hegelian legacy consist? It is also clear that dialectical social theory could hardly be more unfashionable today, even among thinkers in the Marxist tradition. Is the abandonment of dialectics by contemporary theorists warranted? The present work is a contribution to the resolution of these two disputes.[1]

The book is divided into two parts. Part One explores aspects of the Hegelian legacy in Marx's thought. Of course, any reasonably comprehensive account of Hegel's influence on Marx would take many volumes. Here I limit myself to a number of themes that have been either overlooked or dealt with unsatisfactorily in recent scholarship.

Lenin has written that "It is impossible completely to understand Marx's *Capital*...without having thoroughly studied and understood the *whole* of Hegel's *Logic*."[2] However, sections of Hegel's *Logic* have never been adequately examined in terms of their importance to Marxism. I believe that the most important of these sections is that dedicated to the syllogism. Hegel's theory of the syllogism has tremendous significance for the Marxist project, from both a theoretical and a practical perspective. I attempt to establish this thesis in Chapter I.

Turning to Hegel's *Phenomenology of Spirit*, a great many studies have examined the importance of this work for Marx's thought.[3] Most of these studies concentrate on Hegel's account of the Master-Slave dialectic.[4] Hegel's later chapter on religion has been almost completely overlooked. And yet the section in this chapter on the highest form of Greek religion, "the spiritual work of art," is extremely interesting in terms of the Hegel-Marx connection. I argue in Chapter II that Hegel's dialectical progression from the religious ontology presented in Greek tragedy to that found in Greek comedy parallels exactly Marx's move from capital as an alien power to the labor theory of value. An understanding of the logical structure of the former transition can greatly illuminate that of the latter. This chapter builds on the first in that the syllogism is crucial to an understanding of both Hegel and Marx's argument.

The progression in Hegel's *Logic* leading up to the syllogism and the dialectic of Greek religion found in the *Phenomenology* are both essentially *systematic* rather than historical. To what extent did Marx appropriate this aspect of Hegel's thought? There are places where Marx seems to acknowledge clearly that his economic theory is a systematic dialectical theory in the same sense as Hegel's *Logic* or *Phenomenology*. And in other places, he seems to deny vehemently precisely this. In Chapter III, I consider a number of proposals regarding how this apparent contradiction in Marx might be resolved. I then present my own view on the matter.

The first three chapters all consider various aspects of the Hegelian standpoint that Marx incorporated. But any account of the Hegelian legacy in Marx must mention some of the important dimensions of Hegel's thought that Marx rejected. Whereas the social theories of Hegel and Marx both use a systematic dialectic, the content of these theories diverges widely when it comes to the study of generalized commodity production. Richard Winfield's recent work, *The Just Economy*, is very helpful in pinpointing exactly where these divergences lie. Arguing from a Hegelian standpoint, Winfield presents a number of serious objections to Marx's evaluation of market societies. In Chapter IV, I defend Marx's position against Winfield's criticisms.

A great many thinkers reject both dialectical social theory in general and the Hegelian legacy in Marxism in particular. It is hardly surprising that anti-Marxists have taken this position (Böhm-Bawerk and Karl Popper are two typical examples). However today we face a completely unprecedented situation. Hostility to dialectics is now shared by most Marxists and "post-Marxists."[5]

In the debates between anti-Marxists and Marxist defenders of dialectics not many premises are shared. These debates typically degenerate rather rapidly to an exchange of polemics. In contrast, the confrontation between a Marxist defense of dialectics and the Marxist and post-Marxist case against this sort of social theory may be more fruitful. Part Two examines a number of recent Marxist and post-Marxist attempts to argue that the Hegelian legacy is pernicious.[6]

Lucio Colletti, one of the most influential thinkers in Italy today, holds that the most important legacy left to Marxism by German philosophy is to be found in Kant, not Hegel. Chapter V is devoted to an examination of Colletti's case, presented in his *Marxism and Hegel*.

One of the most significant contemporary developments within Marxist theory has been the rise of "analytical Marxism." Although a great variety of perspectives have been lumped together under this heading, most thinkers associated with this movement vehemently reject the Hegelian legacy in Marxism. They hope to replace dialectical social theories with theories based on the methodology of rational choice theory.

The most extensive discussion of this can be found in Jon Elster's *Making Sense of Marx*. In this work Elster presents seven arguments against dialectical derivations of the sort found in the systematic writings of Hegel and Marx. In Chapter VI, I evaluate each of these arguments in turn.

In Chapter VII the topic shifts to John Roemer, another leading figure in the analytical Marxism movement. He, too, rejects the Hegelian dimension in Marx's work. In a series of publications Roemer has presented several serious criticisms directed against the theory of exploitation found in *Capital*. I argue that Roemer's objections all stem from a failure to understand the sort of theory Marx presented there. This in turn stems from Roemer's inability to grasp correctly the methodological approach Marx took over from Hegel.

In most respects "postmodern" social theorists are at the opposite end of the spectrum from analytical Marxists. And yet they agree with analytical Marxists that the Hegelian legacy within Marxism must be rejected. Of course, they hold this position for reasons quite different from those of the analytical Marxists. In Chapter VIII a number of recent essays written by Jean Baudrillard, a leading French postmodernist, are considered from this point of view.

This list of Marxist and post-Marxist critics of dialectical social theory is far from exhaustive. But it is, I believe, representative. A consideration of other critics might change this or that detail. However, the overall picture would not be greatly transformed.[7]

Another point that should be mentioned stems from the fact that there are two distinct species of dialectical social theory. In one, systematic progressions of socioeconomic categories are formulated. In the other, theses regarding the ultimate patterns and fundamental mechanisms of historical advance are proposed. The Hegel-Marx connection is worthy of study in both species. However, in the preceding summary the reader will have noted the relative emphasis of systematic dialectical theory. Chapters I, II, IV, V, most of VI, and VII are devoted to issues connected with this type of dialectical social theory. Historical dialectical theory is discussed in the beginning of Chapter VI and in Chapter VIII. In Chapter III, I ask which species of dialectic provides the underlying architectonic of *Capital* and other economic writings of Marx. I believe that this emphasis is justified in light of the fact that historical dialectics has been discussed more extensively in previous works in this area.[8]

Much of this book is devoted to the explication of the thought of Hegel, Marx and some of their most important contemporary critics. Why should anyone care about these issues? Is anything of more general importance at stake here? I believe that the following study is not a mere exercise in the history of ideas. Issues are discussed that concern the nature of social theory and social practice in general.

In Chapter I two canons for social theory are derived: social theory should be systematic; and it should avoid reductionism. A number of implications for social practice are also discussed: electoral work should not detract from political mobilization; transitional programs must be formulated instead of ultra-Left demands; and class politics ultimately has priority over the politics of particularity. Chapters II and V derive a defense of democratic politics from the dialectical approach. Chapter III argues that a systematic dialectic is important for social theory and practice in that (a) it is an aid to conceptual clarification; (b) it is an aid for overcoming illusions; (c) it is necessary for grounding theoretical claims of necessity; and (d) it is a necessary precondition for any theoretically informed revolutionary politics. In the conclusion to Chapter VI, I return to these themes. In Chapter VIII the limitations of a postmodern politics are explored. The issues at stake in these discussions transcend the narrow concerns of Hegelology and Marxology.

PART ONE

THE HEGELIAN LEGACY IN MARXIST SOCIAL THEORY

I

Hegel's Theory of the Syllogism and Its Relevance for Marxism

In this chapter I examine Hegel's theory of the syllogism. The chapter on the syllogism in Hegel's *Logic* has been mostly neglected by Marxists, and yet it has considerable interest. After some remarks on the *Logic* in general and on the section on the syllogism in particular, I discuss two ways in which this part of Hegel's theory is relevant to the theoretical foundations of Marxism. Then three practical issues are considered, issues that have provoked considerable debate within contemporary Marxism. I argue that Hegel's theory of the syllogism has interesting implications regarding all three issues.

General Reading of the *Logic*

Hegel's *Science of Logic* is surely one of the most difficult books in the history of philosophy. (As a result this chapter is probably the most difficult in the present work.) As we shall see later, a variety of different interpretations have been proposed that attempt to explain exactly what Hegel was up to. In the present section I shall propose the reading I feel best captures Hegel's project. The three basic features of this project will be sketched, followed by some examples that illustrate these features.

Any brief account of the *Logic* is bound to be unsatisfactory in many respects. Those not already familiar with the *Logic* are likely to find the following obscure; and those who are familiar with it will surely find the following oversimplified. My goal is not to provide a complete view of Hegel, but rather to present as simply as possible those aspects of Hegel's *Logic* that are of greatest importance to Marxism.

The Isomorphism of Principle and Principled

In all our theoretical and practical endeavors we continually attempt to make sense of the world. We do this by employing principles. It is possible for us to then reflect on the principles we use, considering them in themselves, apart from any specific application. These principles define general explanatory frameworks. If we think that these principles do indeed help us make sense of the world, then we must hold that the explanatory framework matches the specific framework of what is to be explained.[1] If we term that which is to be explained *the principled*, then we may say that the structure of a principle and the structure of what is principled are isomorphic. The structure of an explanation and the structure of what is to be explained must map onto each other. Once one has been specified the other is specified as well; they are two sides of the same coin.

A principle for Hegel is not simply a category *we* employ to make what is principled intelligible to us. A principle is not to be taken as something merely subjective. It captures the intelligibility of what is principled in itself. In other words, the term *principle* is to be taken in an ontological sense, rather than an epistemological one.

Hegel's *Logic* is made up of a progression of categories. Some of these categories define principles, that is general explanatory frameworks; others define general frameworks of what is to be explained; and still others define both at once.

Different Levels

In the previous subsection I noted that Hegel's *Logic* is made up of a series of categories. How is this series constructed? In answering this question one key point must be kept in mind. Not all principles, and not all ways of categorizing what is to be principled, are on the same level. Some principles are simpler than others, capable of grasping only abstract structures. Others are more complex, capable of grasping more concrete explanatory structures. The same holds for the structures defining what is to be explained. In other words, concrete structures include the structures defined by abstract categories, while simultaneously adding some further content to them. Hegel's *Logic* captures this difference in levels through its systematic ordering of categories. It begins with the categories on the most abstract and simple levels and proceeds in a step-by-step fashion to progressively more concrete and complex stages.[2]

Unity of Unity and Difference

Before turning to some examples to clarify the preceding points, one last bit of Hegelian jargon must be introduced. What is principled is always a manifold, a set of differences. A principle that grasps its intelligibility unifies that manifold in thought. The dialectic of principle-principled thus can be described in terms of a "unity of unity in difference." To say that the dialectic is played out on different levels is to say that there are different ways the unity of unity and difference can be categorized, some more complex and concrete than others.

Examples

These above points can be illustrated with the help of the following categories taken from *Logic*: being; ground and existence; and correlation and actuality.[3]

Being

The category of "being" at the beginning of the *Logic* is the most simple and abstract of all categories. It simultaneously fixes in thought both the most elementary way of employing a principle and the most elementary way of describing what is to be principled. *Being* taken in terms of what is to be principled is what simply and immediately is. When it is taken as a principle, it is the simple assertion that the principled is. In this initial stage in Hegel's progression of categories we have simple unity without any difference.

Ground and Existence

Matters are much more advanced if we skip ahead in the systematic ordering to the level of "ground" and "existence." The former is a type of principle, whereas the latter is a way of categorizing what is to be principled. The structure isomorphic to both can be diagrammed as follows:

When the simple category of "being" is employed, the items in question are viewed as groundless, as simply given in immediacy. Here, in contrast, grounds are to be specified for each individual item in existence. Each existence has its own unique intelligibility, captured in its own set of grounds. Given Hegel's terminology, the pair ground and existence is on a higher level than mere "being" precisely because what exists is mediated through its grounds. It is united with what grounds it, while remaining distinct from these grounds.

On the other hand, the differences among the existences are categorized as immediate within this structure. They are simply given. In other words, the existences are mediated with their respective grounds, but not with each other. In this sense there is difference without unity.

Correlation and Actuality

Two categories found later in the *Logic*, "correlation" and "actuality," specify a different structure.

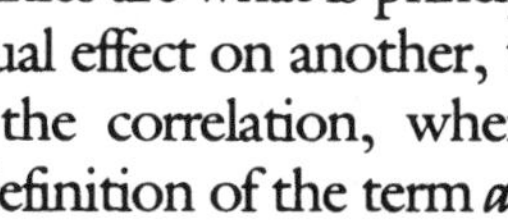

Here the principle is a correlation that mediates a number of different actualities; and the actualities are what is principled. For example, when one entity exercises a casual effect on another, the underlying casual law provides the principle, the correlation, whereas the two entities in question are in Hegel's definition of the term *actualities*. The ontological structure of that which is principled is as follows. The different actualities are not taken in their immediacy apart from each other, as was the case in the framework Hegel defined with the category "existence." Instead each actuality (e.g., that which is the cause and that which is the effect) is what it is precisely through its mediation with other actualities. In this structure we do not have mere unity or mere difference, but rather a unity of unity and difference.

For Hegel it is clear that the principle "correlation" is more complex, more capable of capturing the intelligibility of that which is concrete, than the principle "ground." Similarly, he also held that defining what is to be principled as "actuality" is a more complex way of categorizing it than the category of "existence." Each actuality has its own set of grounds; in addition, it *also* is correlated with other actualities.

Both of these orderings are two sides of the same coin. Both allow a fuller description of the concrete. Any argument that justifies seeing one sort of principle as more complex and concrete than the other simultaneously justifies the assertion that one way of categorizing what is to be principled likewise is more complex and concrete than the other.

The Systematic Place of Hegel's Theory of the Syllogism

There are two basic ways of reading Hegel's theory of the syllogism. The first may be termed *the stuffed dresser reading*. In this view Hegel starts off with the traditional theory of the syllogism with its lists of different syllogistic figures, along with a number of empty "slots" in the architectonic of the system he has contructed. He then proceeds to stuff the different parts of the traditional theory of the syllogism into these slots in his system, as if he were stuffing different sorts of clothing into the different drawers of a dresser. This sort of taxonomic exercise may inspire an admiration for Hegel's inimitable virtuosity in such matters. But it has little intrinsic interest for Marxists (or anyone else for that matter).

Another sort of reading is more fruitful and more in harmony with Hegel's own statements of his intentions. This reading sees the theory of the syllogism as a further stage in the ordering of different structures of principle-principled, with "syllogism-object" being yet more concrete and complex than "correlation-actuality."[4] This reading will be presented here.

For our purposes we do not have to trace Hegel's ordering of the thirteen different sorts of syllogisms. Instead we may move directly to the conclusions of his theory. They will first be presented in fairly abstract terms that may not immediately be intelligible to those not familiar with Hegelian jargon. The examples given in the following section may clarify things.

As a principle the syllogism connects three moments: universality (*U*), particularity (*P*), and individuality (*I*). As principled, objects are individuals mediated by particularities that are essential to them qua individuals, and these particularities in turn are mediated through a universal that is essential to the particularities. As a principle no single syllogism is sufficient to capture the intelligibility of its object. Any attempt to conclude that there is a connection between *I* and *U* through premises asserting a connection between *I-P* and *P-U* leaves these latter assertions unjustified. Likewise any attempt to derive *P-U* from *P-I* and *I-U* leaves the latter two premises unmediated; and any attempt to connect *I-P* through *I-U* and *U-P* treats those premises as simply given immediately. For syllogisms to operate as principles, a system of all three sorts of syllogism is required *I-P-U*, *P-I-U*, and *I-U-P*. Only the system of syllogisms as a whole serves as the principle of explanation on this level of the theory.[5]

There are two key points here. First, each determination is thoroughly mediated with the other two.[6] Second, each determination takes in turn the role of the middle term, whose function is to mediate the extremes into a single totality.[7]

Turning to what is to be principled (the object, in Hegel's sense of the term), Hegel writes that "everything rational is a syllogism."[8] That is, everything intelligible, insofar as it is intelligible, is a "universal that through particularity is united with individuality."[9] The same two features hold for the principled (the object) as characterize the principle (the syllogism). Each determination of the object is thoroughly mediated with the other two. And one cannot claim any ultimate ontological priority for the individual object, or for the particularities essential to it, or for the universal essential to those particularities. Ontologically each of these moments is itself the totality, each equally requires mediation with the other two.

Why does this stage count as an advance over that of correlation-actuality? Correlations capture a mediation that unites different actualities. But some correlations are external to the actualities correlated (e.g., the correlation connecting a rise of mercury in a barometer with a change in weather). Other sorts of correlations are not external. What makes the latter distinct from the former is that external correlations do not stem from the essential nature of that which is correlated. When a mediation is based on the essential nature of that which is mediated, the relation is more complex and concrete than a mere correlation that may or may not be external to what is correlated. A system of syllogisms mediating *I*, *P*, and *U* captures mediations rooted in the essential nature of objects.[10] "Syllogism-object" thus is an advance over "correlation-actuality" from both a conceptual and an ontological standpoint.

Theoretical Importance of Hegel's Theory of the Syllogism for Marxists

The Systematic Imperative

It would be a mistake to believe that substantive theoretical positions can be derived from Hegel's *Logic*, at least in the present reading. The *Logic* consists in an ordering of progressively more complex structures of principles and what is principled. As such it provides a set of canons to follow in theoretical work rather than some magic formula automatically churning out theoretical pronouncements like sausages in a factory. Among these canons are the following. If we wish to grasp a reality in its full complexity and concreteness we cannot simply take it as made up of immediately given beings. Nor can we simply take it as made up of isolated existences with their own unique grounds. Nor can we simply see it in terms of actualities externally mediated with other actualities through various correlations. Instead we must employ a framework in which objects are united in difference with other objects through the essential particularities and universalities that make these objects what they are. This cannot be done through a single assertion or through a series of isolated assertions. It can be done only through a theory in which a number of different sorts of arguments are systematically connected.

The relevance of this to Marxism can be brought out through an example. Marxists generally recognize that one of the key ways Marxist theory is distinct from most bourgeois social theory is its insistence that phenomena not be studied in isolation. A naive bourgeois economist may take a rise in unemployment as something given immediately, as something that just is. This is done for example, when it is identified with a "preference for leisure" that somehow simply just increased. A more sophisticated bourgeois economist might trace a rise in unemployment back to some set of grounds, such as previous demands for higher wages. Yet more sophisticated bourgeois economists treat a rise in unemployment as an actuality to be mediated with other actualities (e.g., a high state budget deficit) through a correlation (such as the thesis that high budget deficits lead to high interest rates, which in turn slow down economic growth and create unemployment). Marxist economists, however, insist that these sorts of accounts at best contain only partial elements of truth. They insist that unemployment can be grasped only in its full complexity and concreteness if it is traced back to the inner structure of capital. It must be seen as an essential manifestation of the logic of capital accumulation and reproduction. In other words, under capitalism unemployment has a necessity to it that most bourgeois approaches to the topic miss. This cannot be established through any single argument. It demands a study of the essential nature of capitalism and the various mediations that connect that nature with an individual occurrence in which rates of unemployment rise. It demands a systematic theory.

What Marxists often do *not* recognize is that in asserting these things they are implicitly accepting Hegel's systematic ordering in the *Logic*, with its move from "being," to "ground" and "existence," through "correlation" and "actuality," to "syllogism" and "object." If Marxist economists were called on to justify in general philosophical terms their methodological approach to the study of a phenomenon such as unemployment, whether they knew it or not they would inevitably find themselves defending Hegel's two isomorphic claims: some sorts of principles are more capable of grasping a concrete and complex reality than others; some ways of categorizing the reality to be grasped capture its concreteness and complexity better than others. To put the point as provocatively as possible: the Marxist approach to political economy is correct *because* Hegel's theory of the syllogism is correct.

Antireductionism

As we have seen, Hegel's theory of the syllogism does not just call for a systematic approach to what is to be explained. In this theory each term, *I*, *P*, and *U*, in turn must take the position of the middle term, constituting the totality that makes the object what it is. This may sound like typical Hegelian nonsense. But it easily can be translated into another important canon for theoretical activity: reductionism must be avoided. I shall first show how this canon is applied in Hegel's own social theory and then turn to its importance in Marxism.

In Hegel's own social theory, the theory of "objective spirit," Lockean individuals possessing both private interests and abstract rights form the moment of individuality; the socioeconomic institutions of civil society provide the moment of particularity; and the state represents the highest level of universality attainable on the level of objective spirit. It is possible to construct three sorts of social theory, each of which is characterized by making one of these moments the middle term mediating the other two into a social totality. This gives us three forms of reductionism. First is the socioeconomic reductionism that comes from reducing individuality and the state to the particular interests of civil society. Social contract theory is interpreted by Hegel in these terms. Second is the methodological individualism that reduces sociopolitical reality to an expression of the private interests of individuals. Finally, there is the political idealism that reduces individuality and the particular interests of society to state imperatives. For Hegel, each of these social theories is based on a syllogism that is one-sided and hence inadequate. What is required is, therefore, a theory that captures the full complexity of the reality here, avoiding all one-sided reductionism.

> In the practical sphere the state is a system of three syllogisms. (1) The Individual or person, through his particularity or physical or mental needs (which when carried out to their full development give *civil* society), is coupled with the universal, i.e. with society, law, right, government. (2) The will or action of the individuals is the intermediating force which procures for these needs satisfaction in society, in law, etc., and which gives to society law, etc., their fulfillment and actualization. (3) But the universal, that is to say the state, government, and law, is the permanent underlying mean in which the individuals and their satisfaction have and receive their fulfilled reality, intermediation, and persistence. Each of the functions of the notion, as it is brought by intermediation to coalesce with the other extreme, is brought into union with itself and produces itself: which production is self-preservation. *It is only by the nature of this triple coupling, by this triad of syllogisms with the same termini, that a whole is thoroughly understood in its organization.*[11]

Of course, no Marxist can accept Hegel's manner of categorizing the sociopolitical realm. State institutions may have a considerable degree of relative autonomy. However, in a capitalist society state institutions will generally tend to further the interests of capital. *Pace* Hegel, the state cannot be categorized as a neutral institution standing above the particular interests of civil society. The interests of capital exert a disproportionate influence on state policy, and this prevents the state from embodying the universality Hegel claimed for it.[12]

Similarly the level of civil society is not, as Hegel believed, simply a realm of particularity in which the particular interests of the agricultural class, the business class, and the class of civil servants are in a fairly harmonious balance (with a small rabble standing off to the side).[13] Within the agricultural class is class antagonism between capitalist farmers and agricultural wage laborers. Within the business class is the same class antagonism between industrial capitalists and industrial wage laborers.

The social theory found in *Capital* from a substantive standpoint thus is quite different from Hegel's. Nonetheless, Marx's analysis also employs a framework taken from the theory of the syllogism in Hegel's *Logic*. It too explores the dialectical mediations connecting universality, particularity, and individuality. In Marx's account, "Capital" is the moment of universality. From the inner nature of capital a number of distinct structural tendencies can be derived. In Hegelian terms these form the moment of particularity. And finally there are the acts of individual capitalists, individual wage laborers, and so on, whose acts are structured by those particular tendencies and thus also mediated with the inner nature of capital.

The logical-ontological apparatus of Hegel's theory of the syllogism is incorporated into Marx's theory, even when Hegel's substantive sociopolitical theory is rejected. It follows from this that the Hegelian canon that reductionism must be avoided is clearly of relevance to Marxists as well. If this interpretation holds, then three forms of reductionism continually threaten Marxist theory. These reductionist options arise when one of the moments (universality, particularity, or individuality) is seen exclusively as the mediating term uniting the other two. First is the reductionism of a capital logic approach. This is a theoretical perspective based on a syllogism in which capital, the universal, is seen as the middle term directly mediating particular structural tendencies and individual acts. Second is the reductionism that dissolves the sociopolitical world into a diverse set of particular structural tendencies. Finally, there is the version of methodological individualism that calls itself Marxist. This standpoint reduces both the inner nature of capital and particular tendencies within capitalism to the intended and unintended consequences of the acts of individuals on the micro level.

Hegel's theory of the syllogism does not save us from the task of examining the strengths and weaknesses of these theoretical perspectives on their own terms. But it does provide reasons for supposing *prima facie* that each position will prove to be one-sided, that each will need to be mediated by the others if an adequate theory is to be constructed, a theory with a concreteness and complexity that matches that of its object. Of course, it would be foolish to think that Hegel's *Logic* could do more than this and show us what such an adequate systematic theory would look like in detail. However the fact that it cannot do all our theoretical work ought not prevent us from from acknowledging the aid it does provide.

In one way or another the chapters that follow all examine Marx's theoretical attempt to mediate the moments of universality, particularity, and individuality together dialectically. In the remainder of this chapter I turn to the role Hegel's theory of the syllogism might play when considering issues of practice.

Practical Importance of Hegel's Theory of the Syllogism for Marxists

Hegel's *Logic* only suggests general canons for theoretical work; it does not provide a ready-made substantive theory Marxists can simply take over. It would be even more foolish to hope that substantive practical evaluations can be derived directly from the *Logic*. Nonetheless, Hegel's theory of the syllogism is not without its practical implications for Marxists, although they must be presented quite tentatively. In the previous section three one-sided theoretical options were sketched: methodological individualism, the capital logic approach, and theories concentrating exclusively on particular tendencies. For each of these options there is a corresponding practical orientation that is equally one-sided. Here too each of these orientations must be examined on its own terms. But here too Hegel does provide us with reasons to regard each one-sided perspective as *prima facie* inadequate.

Let us first take the syllogism underlying methodological individualism, which sees individuals and their acts as the middle term mediating both particular tendencies in capitalism and the system as a whole. An example of a practical orientation that corresponds to this would be an emphasis on the importance of individuals' electoral activity, for example, balloting on political matters and regarding strike actions. What is correct here is the importance granted to the moment of the individuals' consent to political and trade union activity. But what is missing is an acknowledgment of how both the inner nature of capital and particular tendencies within capitalism work to atomize individuals.

Consider a decision on whether to strike made by individuals privately through mailed-in ballots. Here the power of capital over each of them taken separately will generally lead to cautious and defensive voting. But if such decisions were made after a collective meeting in a public space, a space where atomization could be overcome and where a sense of the collective power of the united work force could arise, voting would take on a bolder tone. Workers would be more prone to go on the offensive. Similarly, the practical orientation of building socialism through convincing atomized individuals to pull the correct levers once every few years is one-sided. It cannot substitute for a political mobilization of those individuals aiming at overcoming this atomization.

Let us turn to the syllogism underlying the capital logic approach. Here the universal, capital, is seen as the middle term forming particular tendencies and individual actions into a totality. The practical consequence of holding this syllogism exclusively is ultraleftism. If everything within the society is immediately reducible to a function or manifestation of capital, then the only possible practical orientation for socialists is to step outside society, to be in immediate and total opposition to everything that occurs within it. This practical perspective correctly sees how often measures supposedly designed to reform capitalism end up simply furthering capital accumulation. But a sectarian attitude toward all measures short of the immediate overthrow of capitalist social relations is no answer. That in effect leaves the reign of capital unchallenged in the here and now. It also fails to provide any convincing strategy regarding how to move from the here and now to a point where this reign might be successfully challenged. In other words, this practical orientation fails to see that between *minimalist demands* that are immediately accessible to a majority of people but that in principle do not touch the rule of capital and *maximalist demands* that are not accessible to a majority and therefore also do not threaten the rule of capital are *transitional demands*. These are proposals that the vast majority of people find intelligible here and now, but that ultimately are incompatible with the social relations defining capitalism. They are proposals that are plausible to nonrevolutionaries, but that have revolutionary implications.[14] If the fight for such transitional demands is successful, individuals are educated politically and specific movements are set up that shift the balance of forces away from the interests of capital. In contrast, the ultraleftism calling for the immediate revolutionary seizure of power concerns itself exclusively with the universal. Hegelian logic provides a reason for considering such an undialectical practical orientation as *prima facie* mistaken.

Finally, there is the syllogism that makes the moment of particularity the middle term constituting the society as a totality. A practical exemplification of this syllogism would be the turn from class politics to what might be termed the *politics of particularity*.[15] In this view the struggles against racial and sexual oppression, against environmental degradation and the avoidable harm inflicted on consumers, against the militarization of society, and so on cannot be reduced to the struggle against capital. Accordingly, the women's movement, the antiracist movement, the environmental movement, the movement for consumer rights, the peace movement, and so on ought not to be made subservient to the labor movement. That would ignore the specificity of these movements. And it would be to take one particular struggle, the struggle against class exploitation, and elevate it to a universality it does not possess. From this perspective the attempt to reduce everything to the logic of capital expresses the inherent "totalitarianism of identity philosophy."[16] In this view the unfortunate legacy of Marx's Hegelian heritage leads Marxists to seek an illusory universality at the cost of ignoring the varied particularities that are truly constitutive of the social domain.

A brief digression on Hegel is in order here. The critics of "Hegelian identity philosophy" seem to be unaware that Hegel by no means insisted on there being a moment of identity (universality) always and everywhere. They overlook that in the *Logic* Hegel explicitly included the category of the "*negative infinite judgment*." Within the framework defined by this category the moment of difference, of particularity, is asserted exclusively. He gave as examples statements such as: "The mind is no elephant" and "A lion is no table."[17] Hegel would grant that when one operates on this categorial level, the theory of the syllogism — with its stress on the unity of identity and difference, the mediation of universality and particularity — is *not* relevant. So a global critique of Hegelian identity philosophy" will not wash. Instead the question is whether in the present case the relation between capital and the particular social movements mentioned earlier is like the "infinitely negative" relationship between the mind and an elephant or a lion and a table.

There are two main arguments for insisting that in fact there is difference without unity here, particularity without universality. The first is based on the existence of sexism, racism, environmental damage, and so on in other modes of production besides capitalism. Hence they cannot be seen as merely particular manifestations of an underlying logic of capital.

With this move an ironic dialectical shift has taken place. The defenders of difference, those most against the tyranny of identity philosophy, now turn out to be insisting on the *identity* of the tendencies to sexism, racism, environmental damage, and so on across different modes of production. And now the Marxists insist on the sense in which these phenomena are *different* within different modes. Marxists do not claim that these phenomena are always and everywhere mediated through the logic of capital, but insist that this *is* the case within capitalist social formations. The inner nature of capital is manifested in a tendency to seek divisions within the work force. This furthers racist and sexist social divisions and stimulates the rise of antiracist and antisexist social movements to combat these divisions. The inner nature of capital is connected with a specific tendency for firms to ignore externalities; that is, the social costs of production and distribution that are not part of the internal costs to firms. This leads to both environmental damage and to the production of commodities that impose avoidable harm on consumers. Environmental groups and a consumers' movement are responses to these tendencies. The inner nature of capital is connected to an imperative to employ the resources of the state both to avoid economic stagnation and to ensure that as much of the globe as possible remains a potential field for capital accumulation. The expansion of military expenditures accomplishes both goals, and so militarism too is a particular tendency that arises within capitalism. Peace movements arise in response. The connection between capital and these particular social movements seems quite a bit closer than that between the mind and an elephant!

A second argument for the politics of particularity asserts that viewing the struggle against capital as a principle of unity uniting the different social movements elevates one particular struggle — that of wage labor against capital — to a universality it does not possess. It is true that the labor movement can be (and has been) reduced to a struggle for higher wages, a struggle limited to white men and undertaken without much regard for either the sorts of products made or the environmental damage resulting from producing them. It therefore also seems correct that each social movement should have an independent organization, leadership, press, and so on. Still, it is also true that within capitalist societies the logic of capital tends to generate and reproduce racism, sexism, militarism, and so on; and so the struggles against these tendencies — when pushed far enough — fuse with the struggle against capital. As long as each specific social movement undertakes this latter struggle separately, its chances of success are slim. Progressive social movements must find a way to unite in this struggle against capital, without sacrificing the specificity of each particular struggle. And out of all the particular struggles it is the struggle of labor that confronts capital most directly. It is capital's control of surplus labor that ultimately allows it to generate the tendencies these social movements struggle against. Therefore the struggle of labor can cut off these tendencies at their root. In the terms of Hegel's theory of the syllogism, the syllogism in which particularity is the middle term cannot stand alone, although it captures an important moment of the whole picture. It must be mediated with the other syllogisms. It must especially be mediated with a syllogism that acknowledges how the struggle against capital unites the different social movements, a syllogism in which the moment of universality is the middle term.

No doubt there has never been an activist who opted for political mobilization over exclusively electoral work, or for a transitional program over ultraleft demands, or for class politics over the politics of particularity, as a result of thinking about Hegel's theory of the syllogism! There are political reasons for taking these options that have nothing to do with the general dialectic of universality, particularity, and individuality. Nonetheless, when we try to spell out in philosophical terms what is at stake in such decisions, Hegel can be of help. Hegel insisted that neither a syllogism in which individuality is the middle term, nor one in which universality is, nor again one in which particularity takes that position, is adequate by itself. Only a system of syllogisms in which each is mediated by the others can capture the full concreteness and complexity of the sociopolitical realm. From this we can derive a *prima facie* case for considering some sorts of praxis as superior to others. More than this philosophy cannot do.

II

The Dialectic of Alienation: Hegel's Theory of Greek Religion and Marx's Critique of Capital

The discussion of the relationship between Hegel's philosophy of religion and Marx's thought has concentrated almost exclusively on a single point. Marx, following Feuerbach, rejected Hegel's Christianity on the grounds that it is an illicit projection of anthropological characteristics onto an illusory heavenly realm. For Marx this projection stems from, and covers over, oppression in the earthly realm.[1] Other than this, Hegel's philosophy of religion has not been generally acknowledged to have any special importance for an understanding of the relationship between the two thinkers.

In this chapter I attempt to show that sections of Hegel's philosophy of religion are of considerable interest in other respects as well. I believe that the culminating section of Hegel's discussion of Greek religion in *The Phenomenology of Spirit*[2] ("the spiritual work of art") provides an unsurpassed illustration of a general dialectic of alienation that Marx later took over when he proposed his critique of capitalism. As in the previous chapter, we first must work through an account of Hegel's position before we will be in a position to discuss its implications for Marx's dialectical social theory.

Greek Religion: From Epic to Tragedy

Hegel's philosophy of religion consists of a systematic progression of forms of religion, ordered from that which is the least adequate expression of spirit to that which is the most adequate. Before we can introduce the nature of this progression, we must first ask what the term *spirit* designates for Hegel. Ultimately this is Hegel's term for a dialectical structure of unity-in-difference, in which the moments of universality, particularity, and individuality are mediated together. As we saw in the previous chapter, this structure is so complex that it can never be satisfactorily captured in a single proposition. Only a system of propositions, a set of syllogisms, is adequate to the ultimate ontological structure of spirit.[3]

In the early stages of the progression that makes up his philosophy of religion Hegel considered various forms of religion that are *not* adequate to the ultimate ontological structure of spirit. Some present ontological structures where the moments of individuality and particularity are entirely swallowed up by the moment of universality; in other religious forms the moment of universality is entirely dissipated, leaving only individual differences; and in yet others universality and individuality are harmoniously reconciled, but in an immediate and undeveloped fashion. However, in the logically most advanced forms of Greek religion, the religious world-views expressed in Greek epics,[4] Greek tragedy, and Greek comedy, all three moments are explicitly present. The ontologies underlying these forms of religion can be presented only by means of syllogisms. This means that for the first time in Hegel's ordering of world religions we have forms adequate to the ontological complexity that is spirit. This is why Hegel considered these forms under the heading "the spiritual work of art."

The syllogistic structure of the ontology present in epic poetry can be depicted as follows:

universal = the realm of the gods
particular = the realm of the heroes
individual = the minstrel

Hegel wrote that

> What, however, is in fact present is the syllogism in which the extreme of universality, the world of the gods, is linked with individuality, with the

> Minstrel, through the middle term of particularity. The middle term is the nation in its heroes, who are individual men like the Minstrel, but presented only in idea, and are thereby at the same time *universal*, like the free extreme of universality, the gods. (441)[5]

Although the views expressed in epic poems are more developed than earlier religious forms in Hegel's systematic ordering, they have several serious shortcomings. The universal principles, the gods, present us with an unintelligible jumble of competing claims. No rational principle appears to assign specific tasks to the various gods.[6] Also, the moment of particularity is always in danger of being reduced to the universal moment; it is never clear if the behavior of a hero is really the act of that hero or rather the act of a god operating through the hero in question. The minstrel, representing the moment of individuality, is not incorporated in the epic stories themselves. The poet(s) who initially composed the epic hymns, and the singers who re-create them for later audiences, remain entirely outside the world of gods and heroes. Finally, on a deeper examination the moment of universality is not truly universal. The gods in fact are *not* the ultimate principles of the events that unfold. They are themselves subjected to yet a higher rule, that of Fate, Necessity.

All of these shortcomings are overcome in the form of religion expressed in Greek tragedy. The ontology articulated in this stage of the evolution of religious consciousness has the following structure.

		Necessity (Zeus)	
universal	=	divine law (the Furies)	human law (Apollo)
particular	=	the heroes	the chorus
individual	=	the actors	the spectators

The universal sphere, the realm of the gods, has been subjected to what Max Weber would term a *rationalization process*.[7] In Hegel's own language, "the substance of the divine, in accordance with the nature of the Notion, sunders itself into its shapes, and their movement is likewise in conformity with the Notion" (443). "In conformity with the Notion" means that there no longer is a plurality of gods collected in a haphazard aggregate. Instead we have a rational principle according to which some gods are assigned specific roles derived from the universal law, and the remainder drop away. This universal law is itself a dialectical unity-in-difference. The moment of difference is expressed in the distinction between the divine law and the human law. The divine law is the set of sacred obligations to one's kin. It is the task of the Furies to ensure that these obligations are fulfilled. The human law consists of the set of precepts that form the ultimate basis of the state (what political philosophers will later call the *natural law*). Apollo has the duty of maintaining this human law. But it is not enough that both laws be maintained separately. The two laws are but distinct moments of the one universal law, and it is necessary that they both be maintained as moments of one totality. Zeus embodies this principle of necessity. It is his task to ensure the unity of the universal law in its inner differentiation.

Turning from universality to the level of particularity, there no longer is any confusion regarding who are the agents in the myths being depicted. The heroes act in their own name and accept responsibility for their actions.[8] The chorus that comments on these actions likewise speaks in its own name. Finally, the level of individuality is explicitly incorporated into the religious drama presented in the tragedies. The roles of the heroes and gods are played by flesh and blood human individuals, who take on the masks that represent universal principles (gods) or particular aspects of humanity (heroes).[9] Similarly the chorus represents the point of view of the community of individual spectators of the drama.[10]

The Dialectic of Capital and the Dialectic of Tragedy

At this point we can interrupt our account of these forms of Greek religion and turn to Marx.[11] An examination of Marx's economic theory of capitalism from the standpoint of social ontology reveals that it too articulates a dialectical syllogism:

universal = Capital

particular = $M \rightarrow MOP/LP \rightarrow C^1 \rightarrow M^1$

individual = individual agents

Capital represents a universal principle that is differentiated into a number of particular tendencies. The most basic tendency is for capital to pass through different stages in a circuit of capital accumulation. It first takes on the form of money capital to be invested (M). Investment is then made in the purchase of two different sorts of commodities, the means of production (MOP) and labor power (LP). Labor power is then set to work on those means of production in a production process (P), the result of which is a new sort of commodity (C^1). With luck the produced commodity is then sold for an amount of money that exceeds the initial investment (M^1). When this occurs the circuit of capital has been completed. Capital has been accumulated and can now be reinvested, beginning the circuit anew. (To this set of basic tendencies other particular tendencies can be added, some of which were considered in Chapter I.) Finally, the universal, capital, progresses through the particular moments of its circuits only through the actions of individual men and women acting as investors, wage laborers, consumers, and so forth.

Anyone aware of Hegel's profound influence on Marx will not be surprised at the claim that Marx's theory articulates a dialectical syllogism or that it shares certain features with a form considered by Hegel. However a great number of forms considered by Hegel have a syllogistic structure. Why pick out a stage in his philosophy of religion and claim it has special relevance for Marx's theory? To present an answer to this question we must first turn to Hegel's critique of the ontology articulated in Greek tragedy.

According to Hegel, underneath the surface-level diversity of the various plays is a common deep structure.[12] The central characters believe that they are following the universal law and thus have attained what Hegel termed *universal individuality* (444, 445). But in fact they are following only one aspect of it. They devote their attention exclusively to either the divine law or the human law, either the law of the Furies or the law of the Apollo, either the law of the netherworld or the law of the upper world. They therefore are transgressing the other aspect of the universal law and thus transgressing either Apollo or the Furies.[13] The universal law, embodied in Zeus, must assert itself in the face of this transgression. It does so in the tragic demise of the characters in question. In this manner the complex unity-in-difference of the true universal present in this religious form is asserted, standing in harmony above the conflict between the divine and the human law: "The essence ... is the repose of the whole within itself, the unmoved unity of Fate, the peaceful existence and consequent inactivity and lack of vitality of family and government, and the equal honour and consequent indifferent unreality of Apollo and the Furies, and the return of their spiritual life and activity into the unitary being of Zeus" (449).

When we confront the dramas in this stage of Greek religious life we tend to focus on what befalls the central characters. For Hegel, however, the chorus holds the key to the proper evaluation of this form of religion. In the beginning of his discussion Hegel described the response of the chorus to the unfolding religious drama as follows:

> Where it does detect the earnestness of the Notion in its onward march dashing these figures [i.e., the heroes] to pieces, and then comes to see how ill it fares with its venerated gods who dare to trespass on ground where the Notion holds sway, then it is not itself the negative power which actively interferes; on the contrary, it clings to the self-less thought of such power, [and] clings to the consciousness of an *alien fate*... It is conscious only of a paralysing terror of this movement, of equally helpless pity, and as the end of it all, the empty repose of submission to Necessity. (444-445)

This point is of such crucial importance to Hegel that he repeated it again at the conclusion of his discussion. Referring to the moment of universality he wrote:

> This Necessity has, in contrast to self-consciousness, the characteristic of being the negative power of all the shapes that appear, a power in which they do not recognize themselves but, on the contrary, perish... The simple *certainty* of self, is in fact the negative power, the unity of Zeus, of *substantial* being and of *abstract* Necessity.... Because actual self-consciousness is still distinguished from the substance and Fate, it is partly the Chorus, or rather the crowd of spectators, whom the movement of the divine fills with fear as being something alien. (449-50)

The ontological structure presented in this stage of Greek religion may have the structure of spirit, the dialectical unity-in-difference of universality, particularity, and individuality. However, it does not express this syllogistic structure in a truly adequate form. The moment of individuality, of actual self-consciousness, of the actual spectators of the religious drama, is united with particularity in the form of the chorus that represents it on stage. However, it confronts the moment of universality as an alien force above it, an alien force that asserts its power over individuals with brute necessity. Individuality and universality are not harmoniously reconciled. Hegel therefore insisted that the progression of religious forms must continue until this reconciliation has taken place. Only then will we have attained a form of religion adequate to the essence of spirit.

The language Marx employed in presenting his theory in *Capital* is completely secularized. There is no talk of religion or spirit. Yet Marx's project is similar to Hegel's goal in the philosophy of religion and elsewhere: the evaluation of ontological structures from a dialectical standpoint; that is, from the standpoint of how well they embody a reconciliation of universality, particularity, and individuality. *And Marx's critique of the social ontology of capitalism parallels exactly Hegel's critique of the religious ontology of Greek tragedy*. In both cases the concept of alienation plays a crucial role.

In his systematic economic works Marx presented an ordering of the social forms that make up capitalism.[14] As in Hegel's systematic theories, this ordering consists in a dialectical progression from the most abstract and simple form to those that are more concrete and complex. The main forms in Marx's theory are the commodity form, the money form, and the capital form. In each of these forms an alien force stands over the individuals who fall under it.

In the simplest and most abstract economic category of capitalism, the commodity form, Marx felt that,

> The social character of activity, as well as the social form of the product, and the share of individuals in production here appear as something alien and objective, confronting the individuals, not as their relation to one another, but as their subordination to relations which subsist independently of them.... The general exchange of activities and products, which has become a vital condition for each individual — their mutual interconnection — here appears as something alien to them.[15]

Regarding the money form, Marx insisted that when it is established "the exchange relation establishes itself as a power external to and independent of the producers. What originally appeared as a means to promote production becomes a relation alien to the producers."[16] The same sort of situation is presented on a more complex and concrete categorial level of the capital form. Here, wage laborers represent the moment of individuality over against capital as an alien universal principle: "Its objective conditions, conditions of reproduction, continually confront labour as *capital*, i.e., as forces — personified in the capitalist — which are alienated from labor and dominate it."[17]

It is not possible to consider here whether Marx's substantive claim regarding the social ontology of capitalism is warranted.[18] The point is simply that the social ontology of capitalism presented by Marx has the same structure as that presented in Hegel's analysis of the religious drama found in Greek tragedy. In both cases the moment of universality confronts individuals as an alien necessity above them. The next point to be established is that the dialectical transition beyond tragedy in Hegel's chapter on religion exactly parallels the movement of Marx's theory.

Comedy and the Labor Theory of Value

We can now return to Hegel's account of Greek religion. The shortcoming of the stage of tragedy was that the individual experienced the universal as an alien force. The next advance in the dialectical progression is the assertion of the moment of actual self-consciousness: "The self-consciousness of the hero must step forward from his mask and present itself as knowing itself to be the fate both of the gods of the chorus and of the absolute powers themselves, and as being no longer separated from the chorus, from the universal consciousness" (450). This brings us to the last form of the spiritual work of art, Greek comedy, where "actual self-consciousness exhibits itself as the fate of the gods" (450). The individual actor who had played the role of a god or a hero steps out from behind the mask and "stands forth in its own nakedness and ordinariness, which it shows to be not distinct from the genuine self, the actor, or from the spectator" (450). With this the individual appropriates "the meaning of the inner essence" (451) as its own creation:

> The Fate which up to this point has lacked consciousness and consists in an empty repose and oblivion, and is separated from self-consciousness, this Fate is now united with self-consciousness. The *individual self* is the negative power through which and in which the gods, as also their moments, viz. existent Nature and the thoughts of their specific characters, vanish. At the same time the individual self is not the emptiness of this disappearance but, on the contrary, preserves itself in this very nothingness, abides with itself and is the sole actuality. (452)

In this manner the alienation of a universal force standing over and above the individuals of the community is dissolved:

> Through the fact that it is the individual consciousness in the certainty of itself that exhibits itself as this absolute power, this latter has not lost the form of something *presented to consciousness*, something altogether *separate* from *consciousness* and alien to it.... What this self-consciousness beholds is that whatever assumes the form of essentiality over against it, is instead dissolved in it — in its thinking, it existence, and its action — and is at its mercy. It is the return of everything universal into the certainty of itself which, in consequence, is this complete loss of fear and of essential being on the part of all that is alien. (452-53)[19]

Just as the logic of capital examined by Marx corresponds to the alien necessity ruling over Greek tragedy, so too does Marx's theory include a move that parallels Hegel's move to comedy. *The ontological claim underlying the labor theory of value is the same as that in Greek comedy: we are not subjected to an alien universal essence other than that of our own making.* In comedy we realize that the gods supposedly ruling over us with an alien necessity rest on nothing more than the act of putting on the masks that brings them into existence. We are free to take these masks off, thereby revealing that there is no "inner essence" ultimately separate from our own self-consciousness. In a parallel manner the labor theory of value holds that the social forms appearing to rule over the economy with an alien necessity, that is, the commodity, money, and capital forms, ultimately rest on the act of creating surplus labor. The alien power of commodity, money, and capital is an illusion. It stems from the fact that under capitalism each individual worker confronts the product of the sum total of social labor in isolation.[20] Through their self-association these individuals may come to realize that commodities, money, and capital are nothing more than objectified forms of their own collective labor. This is a comic moment in Hegel's sense. The claim, for instance, that capital is a distinct "factor of production," deserving reward for its "contribution," should be met with laughter. This laughter is the first step toward dissolving the power of these alien forms over the economy.

Hegel on Greek Democracy

I have argued that the path from tragedy to comedy in Hegel's reconstruction of Greek religion exactly parallels Marx's dialectical transition from the rule of capital as an alien force to the self-consciousness that capital is nothing but objectified labor. There is a final parallel to be drawn as well.

Throughout the chapter on religion in the *Phenomenology* Hegel referred to the forms of "actual spirit" that correspond to the stages of religious spirit. At the conclusion of the section on Greek religion Hegel mentioned that the form of socio-political life isomorphic with Greek comedy was Greek democracy.[21] Similarly, for Marx "the association of free individuals," that is, a society in which men and women direct their affairs according to a plan democratically decided on,[22] would count as a systematic advance over a social order based on submission to the alien necessity of the rule of capital.

At this point however, the two paths diverge. Marx affirmed the democratic form, although he acknowledged limits preventing it from being fully realized in circumstances such as those in ancient Greece.[23] For Hegel, in contrast, the problem with Greek democracy did not lie in its limits, but in its very nature. The section on Greek religion in the *Phenomenology* concludes with the following passage. It is worth quoting at length:

> This *Demos*, the general mass, which knows itself as lord or ruler, and is also aware of being the intelligence and insight which demand respect, is constrained and befooled through the particularity of its actual existence, and exhibits the ludicrous contrast between its own opinion of itself and its immediate existence, between its necessity and contingency, its universality and its commonness. If the principle of its individuality, separated from the universal, makes itself conspicuous in the proper shape of an actual existence and openly usurps and administers the commonwealth to which it is a secret detriment, then there is exposed more immediately the contrast between the universal as a theory and that with which practice is concerned; there is exposed the complete emancipation of the purposes of the immediate individuality from the universal order, and the contempt of such an individuality for that order. (451)

Hegel's own sentiments are forcefully presented here. We know from *The Philosophy of Right* that Hegel felt that the culmination of the state is expressed in a monarch who is not democratically elected.[24] The passage is fully consistent with this view.

In Chapter IV I compare the normative model of institutions Hegel affirmed in the *Philosophy of the Right* with Marx's critique of capitalism. In the remainder of this chapter I wish to pursue a question that concerns Hegel alone. Does the above antidemocratic perspective follow from his own dialectical analysis of the concluding stage of Greek religion?

In the preceding passage Hegel derived "the contempt of... individuality for that [universal] order" from the rejection in comedy of a religious essence separate from the community of individuals. But does this contempt necessarily follow from the rejection of the notion of an alien essence? Why is the insistence that the universal order does not have any separate ontological status apart from flesh and blood individuals necessarily equivalent to being "emancipated from the universal order" in general? In other words, need social atomism necessarily result from a denial of alien social forms? Might it not be possible to articulate a universal that is implicit within the community of individuals rather than alien to it?

To answer these questions, let us turn to Hegel's account of Christianity. For Hegel the Christian religion surpasses the level of religious consciousness attained on the stage of the spiritual work of art in one profound respect. In Hegel's reconstruction of the philosophical core of Christian dogma, the trinity doctrine, the relationship between Father, Son, and Holy Spirit is formulated in an explicit system of syllogisms far more developed than anything in Greek religion.[25] In his view this system of syllogisms captures the fundamental ontological structure of spirit. Christianity thus is the form of religion that is fully adequate to spirit.[26] With this Hegel's systematic ordering of religious forms has attained closure.

Whatever one may think about all of this, the point to be made in this context is that there is one respect in which Christianity merely incorporates, without going beyond, the fundamental insight of the stage of Greek comedy. In Hegel's philosophical reconstruction of Christianity, universality has no ontological substance whatsoever outside of the actual community of individuals:

> Spirit remains the immediate Self of actuality, but as the *universal self-consciousness* of the [religious] community, a self-consciousness which reposes in its own substance, just as in it this Substance is a universal Subject: not the individual by himself, but together with the consciousness of the community and what he is for this community, is the complete whole of the individual as Spirit. (462)

Later, when speaking about the crucifixion and resurrection, Hegel wrote that: "the grasping of this idea now expresses... the coming into existence of God's individual self-consciousness as a universal self-consciousness, or as the religious community"[27] (475).

The moment of universality ("universal self-consciousness") thus comes into existence *only* in the community.[28] From this we may conclude that the dissolution of an alien universality need *not* result in "the complete emancipation of the purposes of the immediate universality from the universal order, and the contempt of such an individuality for that order." In Hegel's own terms it can in principle result in an individuality that is reconciled with a nonalien universality within its own community. The critique of democracy Hegel derived in the discussion of the political implications of Greek comedy therefore must be abandoned.

The Marxist project of socialist democracy aims to surpass the democracy that in Hegel's view embodied the "actual spirit" of Greek comedy. Socialist democracy presupposes the material basis of advanced productive capacity; however, it also presupposes *solidarity*. And what is solidarity by a universal principle uniting individuals within a community in a nonalien fashion? There may be reasons for Hegelians to criticize the project of socialist democracy on socioeconomic grounds.[29] However that may be, nothing in Hegel's philosophy of religion mandates rejecting the Marxist project.

I have argued that the development in Hegel from tragedy to comedy and then to Greek democracy helps us understand the development in Marx that moves from a consideration of the various alien social forms in *Capital* to the labor theory of value and then to the call for socialist democracy. Needless to say, from most perspectives there are tremendous differences in the two cases. And from most perspectives these differences would be of the utmost importance. But from the standpoint of dialectical argumentation the logic underlying both cases is identical. The critique of alienation behind both positions is one of the most important dimensions of the Hegelian legacy in Marx's thought. Of course, other places in Hegel's theory illustrate this point. But no other place illustrates this better, and few have been more neglected than Hegel's account of the dynamic of Greek culture.

III

The Debate Regarding Dialectical Logic in Marx's Economic Writings

In Chapter I, I presented a reading of Hegel's *Logic* as a system of categories dialectically ordered from the most abstract and simple to the most concrete and complex. In Chapter II, we saw that the chapter on religion in Hegel's *Phenomenology* also consisted of a sequence of forms systematically ordered according to the same principle.[1] In the previous chapter, I asserted without comment that Marx presented the same sort of dialectical theory in his major works in economics. I claimed that the progression from the commodity form through the money form to the capital form was systematic in the same sense as the Hegelian ordering from "ground" through "correlation" to "syllogism" (or from "epic" through "tragedy" to "comedy"). If this reading is correct, this would be a third significant aspect of the Hegelian legacy in Marx. In addition to the syllogistic framework with the set of theoretical canons and practical recommendations that can be derived from it, and the rejection of alien forms ultimately standing apart from the community, Marx also took from Hegel the general type of theory to be constructed: a systematic ordering of categories.

Whether the Hegelian legacy extends this deeply in Marx is an extremely controversial matter, however. In the first section of this chapter I further develop this reading of Marx and then present three alternative ways of considering Marx's relationship to Hegel on this point. In the second part I present a series of arguments in favor of the claim that Marx took over his general theoretical method in *Capital* and his other major economic works from Hegel.

Four Readings of Dialectics in Marx's Economic Theory

Dialectics as Systematic Categorial Theory

In an 1858 letter to Engels, Marx wrote that "I leafed through Hegel's *Logic* again and found much to assist me in the *method* of analysis."[2] This suggests that Hegel's *Logic* holds the key to an understanding of Marx's methodology.[3] This leads to two questions. What is the method employed in the *Logic*? And how did Marx make use of it?

Some general observations regarding Hegel's philosophy can be added to the remarks made in Chapters I and II. Hegel stated that "philosophy is its time apprehended in thought."[4] Philosophy begins with an appropriation of the fundamental categories underlying the thought of a historical epoch. Its goal is to reconstruct the intelligibility of the world through tracing the immanent logical connections among these pure thought determinations. This reconstruction moves from the most abstract and simple categories to the most complex and concrete. In other words, the ordering of thought determinations is systematic, rather than historical. Dialectical logic is the method that allows us to move systematically from one thought determination to another.[5]

In the "Introduction" to the *Grundrisse* Marx sketched a methodology that corresponds quite closely to Hegelian dialectical logic. The starting point for theory-building for Marx is "the real and concrete" as given in experience. But as immediately experienced it is not possible to have more than a "chaotic conception of the whole" of this experience.[6] Hence, there is a need to proceed to the theoretical reconstruction of that experience. The second stage of Marx's method is to begin with an analysis of the uncomprehended experience through an appropriation of the categories used to make that experience intelligible. The object of experience Marx wished to comprehend was the capitalist mode of production. And so the relevant categories to appropriate are those of everyday experience in this mode of production, those employed by political economists in their attempts to understand this mode of production scientifically, and those corresponding to features of this mode of production previously missed by economists. This appropriation is not a haphazard one. Already a systematic intention is at work. This intention is expressed in the fact that the concepts are worked through with the goal of reaching those that are simplest and most abstract (such as "commodity," "exchange value," etc.) From "a chaotic conception of the whole," Marx wrote, "I would then, by means of further determination, move analytically towards ever more simple concepts, from the imagined concrete towards ever thinner abstractions until I had arrived at the simplest determinations."[7]

Having arrived at the "simplest determinations," Marx continued, "From there the journey would have to be retraced until I had finally arrived at the [concrete], but this time not as the chaotic conception of a whole, but as a rich totality of many determinations and relations."[8] This involves a systematic progression of the appropriated categories. At the conclusion the intelligibility of the intially given concrete will have been comprehended by thought in a systematic fashion:

> The concrete is concrete because it is the concentration of many determinations, hence unity of the diverse. It appears in the process of thinking, therefore, as a process of concentration, as a result, not as a point of departure, even though it is the point of departure in reality and hence also the point of departure for observation and conception. Along the first path the full conception was evaporated to yield an abstract determination; along the second, the abstract determinations lead towards a reproduction of the concrete by way of thought.[9]

This is precisely the thrust of Hegel's approach as well. In moving from abstract categories to concrete ones in a step-by-step fashion the connections, in Hegel's language, are "objectively and intrinsically determined."[10] In Marx's language the goal is to trace "the intrinsic connection existing between economic categories or the obscure structure of the bourgeois economic system... [to] fathom the inner connection, the physiology, so to speak, of the bourgeois system."[11] *This is nothing more than the Hegelian goal of reconstructing the world in thought through working out a systematic theory of categories*. By tracing the "intrinsic connections existing between economic categories" the object realm is reconstructed in thought, the object realm here being the bourgeois system. Marx explicitly acknowledged that this ordering of categories is systematic rather than historical: "It would be unfeasible and wrong to let the economic categories follow one another in the same sequence as that in which they were historically decisive."[12] In this manner the different parts of Marx's theory are united within a single architectonic. They each represent a stage in the systematic progression of categories reconstructing the capitalist mode of production in thought.

The Logicohistorical Reading

When we turn to the "Afterword" to the second German edition of *Capital* we get quite a different picture of Marx's method from that presented in the *Grundrisse*. In the course of a methodological discussion Marx quoted with unreserved approval the following passage from a Russian review:

> The one thing which is of moment to Marx, is to find the law of the phenomena... the law of their development, i.e. of their transition from one form into another, from one series of connexions into a different one.... Marx only troubles himself about one thing: to show, by rigid scientific investigation, the necessity of successive determinate orders of social conditions.... Most important of all is the rigid analysis of the series of successions, of the sequences and concatenations in which the different stages of such an evolution present themselves.

Marx commented, "Whilst the writer pictures what he takes to be actually my method, in this striking and (as far as concerns my own application of it) generous way, what else is he picturing but the dialectical method?"[13]

This version of the dialectical method, however, is the inverse of the dialectical approach found in Hegel's systematic writings. This is why Marx now insisted that he had merely "coquetted" with Hegelian terminology previously.[14] Marx had to stand Hegel on his feet; that is, transform Hegel's "idealist" dialectics into a "materialist" dialectics. It now appears that Marx did not employ a systematic dialectics taken over from Hegel, he instead proposed an alternative. In this reading dialectics is not an ahistorical method of tracing logical connections among pure thought determinations. A materialist dialectic captures the logic of historical development. A materialistically transformed dialectic can thus be termed a *logicohistorical* method.[15] The aim of this dialectic is to eliminate contingent and accidental features of history, thereby revealing the underlying intelligibility of history.

One example from *Capital* can be cited. From this perspective the dialectical transitions from "value" to "cost price" and from "cost price" to "price of production" capture the inner logic of a historical development. The first stage is the precapitalist period of simple commodity production. Here production is undertaken by individuals, none of whom undertakes significant investment in constant capital, *c* (tools, etc.). We therefore may assume that goods and services are exchanged in accord with the labor time socially necessary to produce them. In the second stage, capitalist firms replace individuals as the agents of production. These firms invest in constant capital, but to a fairly limited extent at first. Marx terms investment in constant capital relative to investment in labor ("variable capital" or *v*) the *organic composition of capital*. At this historical stage the organic composition of capital is low in all sectors. We therefore may assume that goods and services are exchanged at their cost prices ($c + v$, plus whatever surplus is generated by labor in the production process). Finally, in a more advanced stage of capitalism some firms have a quite high organic composition of capital relative to others. If we follow Marx in assuming that labor ultimately is the sole source of economic surplus, then if goods and services were to be exchanged at cost prices now the rate of profit would be far higher in labor-intensive industries with a low organic composition of capital than in capital-intensive industries. However if this were to occur investment would surely slow down in the latter sector until the rate of profit increased there. Marx concluded in this reading that in advanced stages of capitalism commodities must be exchanged at prices of production rather than cost prices, with prices of production being those prices that prevent a systematic tendency for a lower rate of profit to beset capital-intensive industries.

This gives us a quite different way to account for the unity of Marx's economic theory. Now each different part of the theory represents a distinct stage in capitalism's logic of historical development, which is clearly incompatible with a systematic reading of Marx's theory.

This presents a problem. Textual justification for both the systematic reading and the logicohistorical reading can be found in Marx. And yet these readings are mutually exclusive. The two remaining interpretations attempt to resolve this problem.

The Development Thesis

Faced with the fact that Marx apparently advocated contradictory positions, some commentators have proposed that Marx's perspective underwent a transformation. In this view his earlier economic writings (*Grundrisse, Critique of Political Economy*) were constructed along Hegelian lines, employing a systematic dialectical logic. He later abandoned systematic dialectics when it came time to write *Capital*, replacing it with a logicohistorical form of dialectical method.

There are two variants of this reading. It is possible to see this shift either as an advance in Marx's position or as a retreat. John Mepham celebrates the alleged development as the manifestation of Marx's coming to maturity as a thinker.[16] In contrast, Gerhard Göhler laments the regression from the "strict dialectics" of Marx's earlier economic writings to the merely "exemplary dialectics" of *Capital*.[17]

The Incoherence Thesis

A final interpretation holds that Marx was thoroughly confused when it came to the question of the methodology that unified his theory. Elements of a systematic dialectical logic similar to Hegel's coexist alongside elements of an evolutionary historical logic closer to Darwin. This is the position Hans-Georg Backhaus ultimately arrived at in his series of significant articles.[18]

It is interesting to note that Backhaus began his series of articles as a vehement defender of the systematic (Hegelian) reading of *Capital*. In his attempt to refute the logicohistorical reading, however, he came to appreciate the significant textual justification defenders of this reading can claim. He therefore concluded that neither reading accounts for the methodological confusion that pervades Marx's writings.

Arguments in Favor of the Systematic Thesis

Against the development thesis I believe that *Capital*, and not just Marx's earlier economic works, follows a systematic dialectical logic. And against the incoherence thesis I hold that *Capital*, along with Marx's other economic works, follows a systematic dialectical logic that betrays few signs of methodological ambiguity. The most satisfactory way to establish this position is to go through *Capital* and the other economic writings step by step, showing how a systematic dialectical logic motivates each transition from one category to another. There is no space to do this here.[19] Instead I shall present a case for the systematic reading in three stages, contrasting it with the logicohistorical reading. First, some internal problems with the logicohistorical reading will be given. Second, I show that certain essential features of Marx's position can be better formulated with the aid of a systematic dialectic. Finally, I conclude with a conjecture regarding why Marx made remarks suggesting that he followed a logicohistorical approach.

Problems with the Logicohistorical Reading

The logicohistorical reading has some plausibility for certain sections of *Capital*,[20] but it can by no means account for the theory as a whole. Consider the sequence "value," "cost price," and "price of production." Each of these categories defines a structure, none of which has ever existed historically. To conceive commodities as being exchanged at their values we must abstract from differences in the time they spend in the circulation process. To conceive commodities as being exchanged at cost prices and prices of production we have to abstract from market demand. Neither of these sorts of abstractions makes any historical sense. In *every* historical phase of capitalism commodities with different circulation times have been exchanged, preventing them from being exchanged at their labor values. In *every* historical period of capitalism market demand has prevented commodities from being exchanged at either their cost prices or their prices of production. In *every* historical stage of capitalism commodities actually have been exchanged according to their "market prices," and "market price" is a category more complex and concrete than "value," "cost price," or "price of production."

This does not mean that Bohm-Bawerk and others who use this as an excuse to abandon Marxism are correct.[21] Marx would insist that any economic theory, like Bohm-Bawerk's, that employs only complex and concrete categories will not take us beyond the surface appearances of economic reality. The categories "value," "cost price," and "price of production" can still function as explanatory principles that capture the underlying intelligibility of the capitalist mode of production, even if they do not capture a succession of historical stages.

A great number of other examples could be given where a logicohistorical reading cannot account for transitions in Marx's theory. A number will be discussed in Chapter VI. Let me mention just one other case here. Consider the transition from a determination at the conclusion of Volume 1, "expanded accumulation," to a subsequent category in Volume 2, "simple reproduction." *Expanded accumulation* refers to the process in which an individual unit of capital generates in its circuit an economic surplus that is then devoted to increased investment in its subsequent circuit. *Simple reproduction* refers to an exchange between the division of the total social capital devoted to producing the means of production and that devoted to the production of the means of consumption. Specifically, this is an exchange in which the economy as a whole continues functioning from one time period to the next in a stable fashion without growth. There has never been a historical process in which the latter grew out of the former. No matter how we formulate the underlying logic of capitalism's historical development, expanded accumulation cannot lead to simple reproduction. For that matter, there never has been a historical example of simple reproduction. The model of simple reproduction may be helpful in understanding essential features of capitalism. But capitalism's inherently dynamic nature rules out the possibility of simple reproduction characterizing a stage in capitalism's historical development.

We are left with only two choices. Either entire chunks of *Capital*, perhaps the greater portion, must be abandoned on the grounds that Marx somehow made amazingly obvious errors in his estimation of the chains of the logic of history. Or we must look for another sort of reason for Marx to have so strongly insisted that "value" be ordered prior to "cost price" and "price of production," and that expanded accumulation" be ordered prior to "simple reproduction." Systematic dialectical logic provides that reason. In Marx's ordering the earlier determinations are simpler and less complex that those that follow. There thus are systematic reasons for their place in the architectonic of Marx's theory.

Strengths of the Systematic Reading

A second sort of argument in favor of the systematic reading over the logicohistorical reading is based on the fact that using the former is more compatible with Marx's fundamental objectives. Three of Marx's most central objectives were to overcome various illusions, to assert certain theoretical claims of necessity, and to ground revolutionary politics theoretically. In all three cases, a systematic theory of economic categories is better suited to attaining these objectives than a logicohistorical sequence of historical stages.

Overcoming Illusions

One of the major illusions Marx fought was the belief that generalized commodity production is somehow "natural." A logicohistorical theory that traced a sequence of stages in which the essential features of commodity production arose could dispel that illusion. But so could a systematic methodology like that presented in the *Grundrisse*, where it is explicitly acknowledged that the categories to be systematically reconstructed are historically specific. Regarding this illusion, then, the two approaches are comparable. But other sorts of illusions are generated within capitalism as well, as Marx made clear in the following passage:

> These same circumstances (independent of the mind, but influencing it), which compel the producers to sell their products as *commodities* — circumstances which differentiate one form of social production from another — provide their products with an exchange-value which (also in their mind) is independent of their use-value. Their "mind", their consciousness, may be completely ignorant of, unaware of the existence of, what in fact determines the value of their products or their products as values. They are placed in relationships which determine their thinking but they may not know it. Anyone can use money as money without necessarily understanding what money is. *Economic categories are reflected in the mind in a very distorted fashion.*[22]

For example, those immersed within historical concreteness inevitably consider "price" and "supply and demand" fundamental economic categories, see the wage contract as a free exchange of equivalents, see "capital" as a productive factor in its own right, and so on. However, Marx held that there is a depth level underlying this surface level of appearances. The task of thought is first to pierce through the appearances to that depth level (the level where "value" is measured by labor time rather than by "price," where exploitation is discovered within the wage contract, where only labor counts as productive of value, and so on) and then to proceed to the mediations that connect the depth level with the given appearances. A logicohistorical sequence of stages does not do this. In contrast, this is precisely what a systematic derivation of categories is designed to accomplish.

Theoretical Claims of Necessity

Most of the claims we make about the world are contingent, and warranted if and only if certain contingent processes can be observed in the world. Such assertions are dependent on observed historical processes in a relatively direct fashion. But some sorts of statements are not meant to be contingent in this sense and therefore cannot have their validity established through a (relatively) straightforward reference to the world.

One of the central ways Marxism differs from other sorts of social theories regards the sorts of statements of necessary connections it finds legitimate. Neoclassical economics, for example, holds that exploitation is a thoroughly contingent matter that occurs only in the more or less exceptional cases where a factor of production is not compensated for its productive contribution; in this sense capital too can be (contingently) "exploited." In contrast, in *Capital* Marx attempted to establish a social ontology in which the structure of capital necessarily includes the moment of exploitation, an exploitation limited to labor.

Consider the difference between the assertion "The owners of this plant exploits these workers" and the statement "capital inherently involves the exploitation of labor." The validity of the first assertion depends on a variety of contingent historical facts about the world: the plant is owned by this person rather than another; it continues operating rather than going out of business; it has these workers rather than those; and so on. The validity of the second assertion depends on there being capital and labor, and this indeed is historically contingent. But once given, capital's exploitation of labor is claimed to hold of necessity, irrespective of specific contingent facts about the world. A theory that wishes to establish a claim of this latter sort therefore must be different than one in which the former sort of claim is made. The goal of the latter sort of theory still is to say something true about the world. But mere historical observation does not establish necessary connections. One cannot jump from statements of the form "This capitalist exploits those laborers," no matter how many, to the assertion that "capital necessarily exploits labor." A different sort of argument and a different sort of methodology is needed.

Here too a logicohistorical approach does not provide an adequate method for attaining Marx's objective. A logicohistorical ordering at best could establish an ideal typical development in which one historical stage characterized by the exploitation of labor necessarily gave way to another stage. It cannot rule out that, in some future stage of the logicohistorical ordering, a nonexploitative form of capitalism might emerge. This is not the same as establishing that capitalism inherently and necessarily involves exploitation. The systematic dialectical methodology constructed by Hegel was developed to defend precisely this latter sort of claim. Categories articulate structures or moments of structures. If reasoning can establish a systematic connection between two categories, say "capital" and "exploitation," this is equivalent to showing that one sort of structure (that captured in the category "capital") is necessarily connected with another (that captured in the category "exploitation"). Systematic dialectical logic, not a logicohistorical form of dialectics, is best suited for establishing necessary categorial connections of the sort crucial to Marx's theory.[23]

Revolutionary Politics

In his economic writings Marx clearly intended to provide a theoretical grounding for a revolutionary perspective. We can distinguish a revolutionary from a reformist perspective in two regards. First, revolutionary politics always are oriented to the long-term goal of changing the fundamental structures of society (however necessary it is to be concerned with transitional goals here and now[24]). In contrast, the reformist is exclusively concerned with changing less than fundamental structures. Second, revolutionary politics against capitalism involve the claim that the fundamental structures to be changed are inherently and necessarily exploitative. The reformist feels that the fundamental structures can be made nonexploitative if they are tinkered with in the right way. On both points a theoretical grounding of the revolutionary perspective requires a systematic dialectical logic.

Revolutionary transformations attack the fundamental structures of a social system. But this requires that we have some way of distinguishing fundamental structures from nonfundamental ones. A logicohistorical method cannot accomplish this task. At best this approach can be used to construct a theory that tells us which structures operate in different historical stages. But the distinction between fundamental and nonfundamental structures can be adequately worked out only within a systematic categorial theory.

Let me present an example. Some feel that measures such as tinkering with monopoly rents through increased state regulations or closely regulating the transactions of financial capital, and so on, constitute a radical step toward socialism. A revolutionary Marxist, in contrast, holds that only a move away from the commodity form, the money form, the capital-wage labor relation, truly counts as a revolutionary transformation to socialism. The theoretical basis for the Marxist position is found in *Capital*. Insofar as the commodity form, the money form, and the capital-wage labor relation are abstract categories serving as principles for the derivation of further categories in a systematic reconstruction of the capitalist mode of production, they articulate structures and structural tendencies that define that system. This implies that transforming other tendencies, thematized in the systematic reconstruction by later, more concrete, categories, leaves the heart of that system intact. Without dialectical logic establishing this connection — a connection that is, by the way, verified practically in the continuous failure of regulations regarding monopoly profits and bank transactions to significantly transform the capitalist system — conscious revolutionary action guided by theory would be impossible. Directionless, ad hoc, spontaneous, and ultimately useless reactions would be the only practical response to capital. A dialectical theory of categories is a condition of the possibility of conscious revolutionary transformation (which, of course, is not to say that it is a sufficient condition).

Turning to the second area of debate between the revolutionary and the reformist, the reformist argues that the shortcomings in generalized commodity exchange are not inherent in the capital form itself. They are due only to contingent conditions. The reformist argues that if only these conditions could be changed (through state regulations, nonadversarial work relations, or whatever) then in principle these shortcomings would be overcome. As I noted in the preceding subsection, the logicohistorical approach leaves this an open possibility. Given any logicohistorical account of exploitation in past stages of capitalism, the reformist always can assert the possibility that the next stage in the historical progression will be characterized by a nonexploitative variant of the capital form. In contrast, Marx's position was that the problems lie with the capital form itself, and not with any set of specific historical conditions. Only the revolutionary transformation of that form adequately can address these shortcomings. To justify this position theoretically Marx had to establish that exploitation is inherent in and necessarily connected to the value form. An examination of prior historical stages does not provide a basis for asserting necessary and essential connections of the sort required. Systematic dialectical logic does, for it allowed Marx to deduce the category "exploitation" from "capital."

A Closing Conjecture

This still leaves the question why Marx at times endorsed a nonsystematic reading of his later economic works. My own conjecture is that this must be seen in the light of public response to the publication of *A Critique of Political Economy* and the first edition of Volume 1 of *Capital*. In the history of the socialist movement no works have ever been as eagerly anticipated. However, it is also the case that no works have ever been greeted with more disappointment. Marx himself had assimilated systematic dialectics, and he gave himself a refresher course on Hegel's

Logic just prior to writing *Capital*. But the reading public had changed by the time *Capital* was published. The Hegelian movement was dead. The audience Marx wanted to reach simply was not familiar with the systematic approach to ordering economic categories.

At this point Marx had two options. In subsequent editions of *Capital* he could have anticipated Lenin's famous aphorism and insisted that no one could fully understand this work without a prior understanding of Hegel's *Logic*. If he had taken this tack *Capital* would surely have remained a significant work in intellectual history. But it is doubtful it would have attained world historical significance. And so he took the second option. He downplayed the systematic nature of the theory and stressed the much more accessible historical components of the work.

He could do this without bad faith for three reasons. First, the book does contain historical theses and illustrations that can immensely profit those who lack all knowledge of Hegel and have no interest in the logic that generates Marx's systematic theory of economic categories. Second, Marx had a metaphysical reading of Hegel. He interpreted Hegel's "absolute" as a metaphysical supersubject that generated itself out of itself, while overlooking those passages where Hegel asserted that philosophy is nothing but its time apprehended in thought. If this interpretation is granted, then Marx would have been quite correct to contrast the historical starting point of his own theory to Hegel's position. Finally, the ultimate purpose of Marx's theory is to contribute to historical change. In contrast, Hegel's ultimate purpose was to reconcile us to the rationality of the present.[25] In this sense Marx's position is historical in a sense that Hegel's is not. None of this changes the fact that a systematic dialectical logic taken over from Hegel provides the architectonic of *Capital*.

IV

Hegel and Marx on Civil Society

The first three chapters of this book have focused primarily on methodological matters connected with dialectical social theories of Hegel and Marx. It is now time to turn to more substantive issues, although as we shall see the methodological and the substantive by no means can be completely separated. For our purposes the relevant substantive issues can be grouped under three general headings: the "idealism" versus "materialism" debate, the role of the individual, and the analysis of socioeconomic structures. The first two issues form the topic of the next chapter, the last provides the topic of this one.

On the socioeconomic plane the significance of Hegel for Marx's thought is considerable. For instance, Hegel's analysis of the work process stressed both the creative role of human labor and the importance of the means of production in a manner that Marx later repeated.[1] And Hegel first derived structural tendencies in capitalism toward relative immiseration, the formation of the reserve army of the unemployed, and the concentration and centralization of capital.[2] However, at the conclusion of Chapter II, I suggested that the social theories of Hegel and Marx ultimately diverge. This raises two questions. Is it indeed accurate to see a substantive disagreement between the two thinkers here? And if there is a divergence, whose position is more compelling?

A point-by-point comparison of *The Philosophy of Right*, Hegel's major contribution to dialectical social theory and *Capital* and other key works by Marx would demand a book of its own. Fortunately two recent books help make the task here more manageable. David MacGregor's *The Communist Ideal in Hegel and Marx* and Richard Dien Winfield's *The Just Economy* raise the issues most germane to the present context in a succinct fashion. I introduce the key substantive differences between Hegel and Marx through a critical examination of these works.

A Convergence?

David MacGregor defended two quite strong claims regarding Hegel's social theory vis-à-vis Marx's. First, he wants to show that Hegel explicitly formulated *every* significant thesis defended by Marx: "Marx did not transcend Hegelian philosophy, he merely developed and amplified ideas already available in the discussion of civil society in the *Philosophy of Right*."[3] In MacGregor's view, for example, two of the most important claims in Marxism, the labor theory of value and the thesis that the means of production should be owned collectively, are simply taken over from Hegel. This is not more widely known because "Marx is less than honest either with his readers or with himself"[4] regarding the depth of Hegel's influence. Second, MacGregor claimed that on two central issues, the transition to communism and the nature of the communist model, Hegel developed the implications of the "Marxist" position better than Marx himself did. Neither of these claims is plausible.

First, MacGregor was able to equate the Hegelian and Marxian notions of *value* only by assuming that because they both used the same term they must mean the same thing. Hegel, like Marx, realized that the value of a commodity abstracts from its specific qualities. However Hegel did *not* state that what remains from this abstraction is abstract labor, as Marx did. For Hegel the common element that allows us to exchange commodities is that fact that they demanded.[5] Hegel's theory of value thus anticipated marginal utility theory, which derives economic value from the relation of demand to supply, much more than Marx's labor theory of value.

Hegel also asserted that possession of a thing requires forming or using it.[6] From this assertion MacGregor extrapolated to the thesis that Hegel holds that those using means of production should own them. The problem with this extrapolation is that the text in question is not being read in its systematic context. It is taken from the first section of the *Philosophy of Right*, "abstract right." This section discusses the manner in which isolated individuals express their own will on external objects and the degree to which this expression is acknowledged by others. In other words, Hegel was operating on an extremely abstract level here, a level *prior* to the introduction of social institutions into the theory. Although Hegel believed that in a situation without social institutions use grants the right to possession, we cannot conclude that he held that the means of production should be owned by those who use them once institutions have been introduced into the theory. As we noted in earlier chapters, later categories in Hegel's systematic ordering go beyond earlier ones in concreteness and complexity. This means that what held for abstract and simple levels of the theory may not continue to hold in later stages. Hegel in fact stated that one's lot in civil society (i.e., after socioeconomic institutions have been introduced) is a function not just of one's skill and luck, but also of one's unearned capital.[7] He would not have asserted this if MacGregor's interpretation were accurate.

Second, we can now turn to the places where MacGregor claimed that Hegel developed the essence of the "Marxist" position in a manner that surpassed Marx himself. In the first area, the transition to communism, MacGregor's account presupposes a commitment to reformism. He correctly stresses that Hegel called for many reforms in the workplace (health and safety plans, grievance appeals, educational and retirement packages, flexible hours, job enrichment, worker involvement in management). As a result MacGregor concluded that in Hegel's model "corporations are slowly being transformed into institutions of workers' control and direct democracy" in a manner Marx failed to anticipate.[8]

Marx, however, had good reasons to question the scenario of what MacGregor describes as the "abolishment of alienation within capitalism itself."[9] Despite the sorts of reforms Hegel mentioned, corporations retain weapons such as the threat of capital strike and actual disinvestment strategies. These weapons will be used whenever reforms significantly threaten their control over the workplace.[10] This would force either a rescinding of the reforms or direct action on the part of the workers to extend them (seizure of factories, etc.). If the former occurs, then there would be no transition from capitalism to worker's democracy. If the latter takes place, then the transition would be really a revolutionary rupture. This is not the dynamic sketched by Hegel. Hegel does not develop a "Marxist" position past the point at which Marx left things; he presents another position altogether.

Finally, MacGregor asserts that "objective mind in its full development (i.e., Hegel's theory of the state) is really only Hegel's term for what Marx later called communist society,"[11] presented in a much more detailed fashion than in Marx. But this is a strange form of communism indeed, in which the essence of capitalist class relations (e.g., treating labor power as a commodity that the members of one class sell to another[12]) remains.

Hegel's model does have an astonishing relevance to contemporary discussions. But it is a predecessor not of a communist society, but of the neoliberal Utopia wherein government, business, and labor cooperate in a stable system of capitalist production. As MacGregor's own discussion makes quite clear, Hegel's goal is a state that *harmonizes* class differences. This is not simply a more-detailed presentation of Marx's notion of communism. It is an idea fundamentally different from that of *abolishing* class differences.

The Divergence

In *The Just Economy* Richard Dien Winfield examined Hegel's systematic ordering of sociopolitical categories in *The Philosophy of Right* in great detail. He forcefully defended the ultimate validity of Hegel's standpoint. Winfield was especially interested in the category "civil society." Here Hegel provided a normative theory specific to the economic realm. The central normative principle is civil freedom. This is the right to choose to develop conventional needs that can be met only through entering into reciprocal agreements with others, who likewise are meeting their freely chosen needs through mutual agreement. Winfield traced how Hegel derived a normative justification for market transactions, socioeconomic interest groups, and public regulatory bodies from this starting point. This part of the book is an interpretive *tour de force*. Winfield carefully unpacked Hegel's argumentation where it is compressed, he clarified where Hegel was obscure, and he drew out implications of Hegel's position that Hegel himself passed over.

But Winfield was no mere apologist. He did not hesitate to correct Hegel where he believed that Hegel was mistaken. Before returning to Hegel-Marx comparisons, some of these corrections should be mentioned briefly. Winfield found Hegel's theory of estates seriously flawed. It included two groups that do not exercise civil freedom: participants in subsistence agricultural production (landlords and peasants: the "natural estate") and public officials. Also, Hegel lumped all the various modes of exercising civil freedom into one estate (the "reflective estate"). This theory of estates must be replaced with a theory of classes, in which different modes of exercising civil freedom can be distinguished.

On the political plane Hegel is to be faulted for reducing the legislative division of the state to the representation of the interests of the natural and reflective estates. This undermines Hegel's claim that the state stands on a higher categorial level than civil society.

Another set of corrections involves the categories "corporations" and "police." The former results from the free decisions of autonomous economic agents to enter groups to protect their interests. The latter involves public regulations that provide for the general preconditions for exercising economic freedom. From a systematic standpoint the latter is a more complex and concrete determination. Winfield therefore correctly concluded that Hegel should have presented it later in the systematic ordering of categories. And he felt that Hegel did not anticipate the wide variety of interest groups that may fit under the heading of corporations.

Hegel also had a far too restrictive view of public regulations. Hegel began with the supposition that, if there were no civil society, nature and the family would provide individuals with their subsistence needs. Whenever the market transactions of civil society threaten the satisfaction of an individual's subsistence needs, Hegel continued, public authorities have a duty to take over the role nature and the family play when civil society is not present. Public authorities must ensure that subsistence needs are met. Winfield responded that civil freedom involves the development of conventional needs that transcend natural subsistence needs. If civil society is to function in a just manner, public regulations must provide individuals the opportunity to attain these conventionally defined needs, rather than mere subsistence.

Finally, it is well known that Hegel saw imperialism and colonialism as forms of public regulation that serve the interests of economic agents. Winfield pointed out the irrefutable fact that Hegel here undermined his own normative principle of right.

Despite these corrections, Winfield's main objective is to defend the essential features of the Hegelian account of civil society. Most important for our interests, at each stage in his presentation of Hegel's systematic theory Winfield considered and rejected the theoretical alternative suggested by Marx. I would like to concentrate on his four central objections to Marx. These have been selected on the grounds that they raise issues that go to the heart of a comparison of the dialectical social theory in Hegel and Marx.

First, Winfield accused Marx of confusing the natural and the social throughout his writings. This category mistake occurs when Marx defined economic use values in terms of natural needs: "Marx describes use value as the relation of the particular natural features of a desired object to the particular natural needs of some human being."[13] It can be found also in Marx's naturalistic definition of abstract labor: "Abstract human labor power and socially necessary labor time are characterized in technical terms completely extraneous to the transactions that supposedly first bring private producers into social contact and thereby render their labor socially universal."[14] But use values meet conventional needs, defined in a social context and capable of being multiplied indefinitely. Likewise laboring is a social activity, not a technical relation between a private individual and nature. Therefore Marx's theory, unlike Hegel's, cannot provide much assistance to a theory of socioeconomic justice.

To some extent this can be dismissed as merely a very questionable reading of Marx. After all, Marx did write that

> The discovery, creation and satisfaction of new needs arising from society itself; the cultivation of all the qualities of the social human being, production of the same in a form as rich as possible in needs, because rich in qualities and relations — production of this being as the most total and universal possible social product, for, in order to take gratification in a many-sided way, he must be capable of many pleasures, hence cultured to a high degree — is likewise a condition of production founded on capital.... The development of a constantly expanding and more comprehensive system of different kinds of labour, different kinds of production, to which a constantly expanding and constantly enriched system of needs corresponds.[15]

So human needs are *not* limited to biological necessities in Marx's account.

Turning to the question of labor, for Marx abstract labor is defined in terms of *socially necessary* labor. This means that all attempts to define Marx's category in technical terms alone are doomed to fail. Socially necessary labor cannot be defined for Marx independent of the social exchanges that determine whether the commodity in question is a social use value: "Nothing can have value, without being an object of utility. If the thing is useless, so is the labour contained in it; the labour does not count as labour, and therefore creates no value."[16] In his discussion of both needs and labor Marx did not confuse social forms with natural forms.

It is true that there are passages where Marx discussed use value and labor in naturalistic terms. But we should not be too quick to conclude that category mistakes were made. The question of the linearity of dialectical theories should be considered first.

A dialectical theory is a systematic progression of categories that moves in a step-by-step fashion to progressively more advanced determinations. As I argued in the previous chapter, this holds for *Capital* no less than for *The Philosophy of Right*. Each succeeding determination goes beyond the preceding ones. Winfield was quite correct to insist that a category on the relatively advanced level of "civil society" cannot be reduced to a determination on the earlier level of "nature." On the other hand, each later category also in some sense "sublates" those that have gone before. Even though the linearity of the theory forces us to consider one category at a time, each categorial level is overdetermined. It is determined not just by the new categorial elements introduced, but also by the preceding determinations incorporated in the new stage.

When Marx pointed out that the capacity to develop needs and to labor is natural to the human species, this does not necessarily imply that he was guilty of confusing the natural and the social. He was simply asserting the overdetermination of the social level, based on its sublation of the natural. From the standpoint of dialectical methodology this is quite legitimate in principle.

A second objection to Marx proposed by Winfield involved two presuppositions: the first is a socioeconomic thesis regarding market societies; the second, a principle of dialectical methodology. The socioeconomic thesis affirms that the economic freedom of those engaging in commodity exchange makes the results of economic activity indeterminate:

> What makes commodities exchangeable are the concurring decisions of their respective owners, who are independent market agents, free to decide what they need and how they will dispose over their own commodities. In entering the transactions through which exchange value is determined, they need not be swayed by any particular external consideration, nor follow any putative model of economic rationality."[17]

The methodological thesis was not stated explicitly by Winfield, but it is implicit throughout his critique of Marx. It states that a dialectical transition from one socioeconomic category to the next can claim systematic necessity only if all agents necessarily act in the manner specified by the new determination. Whenever it is logically possible for some economic agents to not act in the specified manner, then the transition is not justified.

Putting these two theses together we can formulate the following general argument. At crucial junctures of his theory Marx ignored the freedom of those engaged in commodity exchange. He claimed that transitions from one category to another were systematically necessary, when in fact the freedom of economic agents makes it possible for them to not act in the manner specified by the new determinations. Therefore Marx's systematic ordering of economic categories cannot be accepted. Marx failed to provide an adequate theory of the just economy.

There are three cases where Winfield employed this argument. In each case Marx presented a view of civil society diametrically opposed to the Hegelian position defended by Winfield. First, Marx derived the labor theory of value from commodity exchange. But the partners in a commodity exchange are free to trade at prices mutually agreed on. To limit their exchanges to prices regulated by labor values ignores this freedom: "Market freedom determines the exchange value of commodities through the actual agreements effecting their exchange, irrespective of any labor expended in antecedent production processes or any qualities intrinsic to the goods themselves."[18] Second, Marx derived the category of exploitation from the capital form. But the wage contract also rests upon a reciprocal agreement of wills. To assert that it is inherently exploitative ignores the freedom of these wills: "Commodity relations do not entail any exploitation of their own, whereby certain individuals are subject to the unilateral will of others by dint of market forces alone. . . . The agents in question all fill their class roles by exercising the same interdependent autonomy at work in every commodity relation."[19] Finally, Marx went on to derive from the capital form the position that capital is an overarching force that subsumes commodity exchange under it as a subordinate moment. But there is no guarantee whatsoever that capitalists will obtain the profits they seek. They will obtain profits only if other economic agents, their suppliers and consumers, agree to trade with them at the right sort of prices. And these other agents are free to not agree to do so. Granting the holders of capital overarching power ignores the fact that civil freedom makes all profit-seeking precarious: "Any consideration of economic justice will go awry unless it keeps in mind that capital cannot escape the influence of factors exogenous to its own dynamic of accumulation, yet endogenous to the market economy in which each and every form of capital plays a component role."[20]

Interestingly enough, what I have termed Winfield's *socioeconomic thesis* is not controversial from a Marxist standpoint. Marx did not regard the freedom of commodity exchange as illusory. He, following Hegel, felt that this was a major factor in the fact that capitalism counts as a historical and moral advance over earlier modes of production such as slavery and serfdom. In contrast, however, the methodological thesis is extremely controversial.

Socioeconomic categories define fundamental socioeconomic structures. As structures within which the freedom of the will is manifested, these structures allow for a multitude of individual occurrences. Nonetheless structural parameters may constrain individual decisions. If so, it may be the case that certain structural tendencies are present. These tendencies may hold through, rather than despite, the free choices of agents operating under these parameters. Winfield himself granted this when he stated that the "ubiquitous element of market freedom does not preclude the working of definite laws governing the individual and global consequences of exchange transactions."[21]

The question we now must pose concerns the appropriate topic for categorial analysis. Is it the myriad contingent choices that individuals might possibly make, were they to act within the structure defined by a given category? Or should our interest be directed instead to the general structural tendencies that hold on the given categorial level? I believe that the former is a matter for individual biography, whereas the latter is the proper concern for dialectical social theories. And I believe that this was Hegel's position as well.

Consider the category "property" in *The Philosophy of Right*. This defines a structure within which persons objectify their will in external objects. On the level of individual biography, persons are free to do this in a harmonious fashion. Yet the structural parameters of the situation — on this level of abstraction persons are motivated by self-interest alone and no legal framework is present — necessarily lead to a structural tendency for nonmalicious wrong, fraud, and crime to arise.[22] Hegel used this as a basis for arguing that the move from the category "property" to the category "crime" was systematically necessary. He proposed this transition despite the fact that it is logically possible for persons to refrain from engaging in the behavior specified by the latter determination.

When we turn back to the three transitions defended by Marx with this in mind, Winfield's objections lose much of their force. On the level of individual biography it is certainly the case that individuals may exchange commodities without regard for labor productivity. But the structural parameters defined by Marx's category of commodity exchange — self-interested agents, abstraction from complicating factors such as different commodities having different circulation times, imbalances in supply and demand, and so on (factors that Marx introduced at more concrete stages of the theory) — still may ensure that on this level of abstraction it is necessarily the case that there is a structural tendency for exchange to be regulated by the productivity of labor. Similarly, on the level of individual occurrences it may be possible for wage laborers and capitalists to agree on wage contracts that are not exploitative. But the structural parameters of the situation — one group owns or controls both the productive resources of society and considerable reserve funds for personal consumption, whereas the other does not — still may ensure that a structural tendency arises in which this is not the case. Finally, it is true that under conditions of legality capital can be accumulated only when suppliers of input and consumers make certain sorts of free decisions. Marx recognized this fact with the category of "market prices" in Volume 3 of *Capital*. However, this merely explains why one unit of capital rather than another survives. It may still be the case that on the macro level of capital in general there is a structural tendency for the concentration and centralization of capital. As Winfield himself stressed, all units of capital "face the market imperatives of having to reinvest and expand simply to survive in face of advancing competition."[23] In Marx's view the structural tendency for capital to subsume commodity relations is nothing more than the result of this imperative for units of capital to expand.

I certainly have not proven here that the structural tendencies discussed by Marx can be established.[24] But I have shown that it is possible to affirm the necessity of structural tendencies arising without denying capriciousness on the level of individual choice. If the necessity for a categorial transition can be defended in terms of necessary structural tendencies, then Winfield's objections miss their mark. In principle the transitions defended by Marx in *Capital* may be as warranted as the transition from "property" to "crime" in Hegel.

A third objection involves what may be termed *categorial universality*. Winfield held that at three central places in *Capital* Marx's theory lacks this essential component.

Marx moved from commodity exchange to the labor theory of value. But the labor theory of value is relevant only to commodities that have been produced. Not all commodities need to be produced. Found objects, land, and so forth also can be exchanged. Hence Marx's discussion of commodity exchange lacks categorial universality:

> Like all labor theories of value, Marx's conception takes for granted that commodities are all produced. By making this assumption, he commits the fundamental category mistake of conflating the genus commodity with the particular class of commodities that are products, while treating features germane to the latter as if they were constitutive of qualities common to commodities in general.[25]

A similar point holds for the investigation of capital. In attempting to account for how the money the capitalist ends up with (M^1) can exceed the initial capital invested (M), Marx limited his discussion to capital invested in the production of commodities: that is, to the $M \rightarrow C \rightarrow P \rightarrow C^1 \rightarrow M^1$ circuit of capital. (C = commodities purchased as inputs of production; P = the production process; C^1 = the produced commodities that are then sold.) Marx held that only an examination of the production process can account for the gain that constitutes capital. But gains can be won by capitalistic merchants who do not concern themselves with production at all. It is also possible for financial capitalists to win gains in transactions that do not involve produced commodities. Winfield wrote, "the basic interaction of capital need not rest upon any intervening production process, but may simply involve speculative buying and selling.[26]

Finally, in his discussion of capitalist industrial production Marx limited his analysis to production undertaken by laborers who have hired out their labor power to the private owners of firms for a wage. But this is just one of a number of different ways capitalist production can be organized:

> Just as commodity relations permit any market agent, from individual to state, to play the role of "capitalist," so they enable commodity producing capital to take any form the market permits, be it a private business whose owner is the sole employee, a worker co-operative whose members draw dividends rather than wages, a share-holding corporation whose employees receive stocks as well as wages, or a state enterprise employing wage labor.[27]

The theory of capitalist production constructed by Marx ignores these different possibilities. Hence it too lacks the categorial universality required by an adequate theory of economic categories.

Let us examine the notion of categorial universality more closely. One could argue that the term is not univocal; the same category can be used in different theoretical contexts. It is possible to distinguish employing a category as a genus from employing it as a determination in a dialectical progression of categories. It could well be the case that the appropriate notion of universality is different in these two different contexts.

The universality appropriate to a genus is characterized by inclusivity. By this I mean that it would be mistaken to consider some of its species in a manner that implied that other of its species are to be excluded from membership in the genus. Consider the category "deception" taken as a genus. Under this heading fall diverse species ranging from self-deceptions regarding one's accomplishments to deceptions regarding the terms of a contract exchanging external objects. Any attempt to define the category would be illegitimate. However when we examine the same category from the standpoint of a dialectical progression of categories things appear differently. It is possible that species that must be treated together *qua* instances of the same genus fall on different levels from a systematic standpoint. Some of these species may embody structures that are relatively abstract and simple, whereas others may manifest structures that are more complex and concrete. In Hegel's *Philosophy of Spirit*, for example, individual self-deception falls on the level of Subjective Spirit. From a systematic perspective it thus must be ordered prior to deceptions regarding contractual exchange, a determination on the level of Objective Spirit ("fraud").

Armed with this distinction it may be possible to mount a defense of Marx against Winfield's attack. Marx can be defended if there are plausible reasons for asserting that different species of commodity exchange and capital fall on different levels from a systematic standpoint. Such reasons can be provided.

If we treat "commodity exchange" as a genus, then exchange involving produced items is simply one species of exchange among many, with no special theoretical privilege over the others. Marx certainly was aware that other species of exchange exist. He talked of commodities that have a price without having a value, including under this heading commodities that are exchanged without having been produced (this would come as a great surprise to readers of Winfield's book who were not familiar with *Capital*). But Marx's theoretical objective was not the enumeration of the species of commodity exchange. It was rather the dialectical reconstruction in thought of the categories that capture the intelligibility of a specific mode of production. From this systematic perspective different species of commodity exchange may fall on different levels. I have already noted that both Marx and Winfield agreed that the indefinite multiplication of conventional needs is an essential feature of market societies. This implies that the exchange of nonproduced items, of commodities that have not been transformed in any manner in response to this indefinite multiplication of needs, necessarily is a peripheral matter in societies based on generalized commodity exchange. The production of commodities for exchange therefore is essential to generalized commodity exchange in a way that exchange of found objects is not. Hence Marx had a strong reason for treating the former prior to the latter in his systematic ordering of economic categories.

Similarly, if we treat "capital" as a genus the circuit of capital that involves production is just one species of capital among many, with no special theoretical privilege over the others. Here too Marx was well aware of the existence of different species. Hundreds of pages in *Capital* are devoted to the analysis of merchant capital, financial capital, rent, and other species of the capital circuit (this too would come as a complete surprise to someone whose knowledge of Marx came from Winfield alone). But in this case as well it is possible in principle that these diverse species do not all fall on the same level from a systematic perspective. The growing number of non-Marxist economists who insist that economies in which capital is invested predominantly in speculative transactions are not healthy might be mentioned in this context. This at least suggests that Marx's insistence that this species of capital is secondary from a systematic point of view is not without some plausibility.

Finally, regarding labor within capitalist production, Marx was fully cognizant of species other than wage labor hired by private capital (yet another point that Winfield failed to mention). But he held that it would be mistaken to see them as all being on the same categorial level. The social relation in which nationalized capitalists firms hire laborers involves the state. Hence, from a systematic standpoint it would be illicit to consider it on an abstract level of the theory where the state had not yet been introduced. Marx likewise was well aware of the possibility of self-employment. However, he felt that the dominant structural tendency to concentration and centralization (a tendency that Winfield granted) implies a tendency for this form of labor to be of peripheral importance. From this Marx concluded that it was legitimate to abstract initially from this species of capitalist production. Regarding workers' co-operatives, Marx saw them as extremely complex. On the one hand, he agreed that they are a species of capitalist production; however, he also felt that they include elements that point away from the capital form. Therefore, he considered them at a very late stage in his categorial reconstruction of the capital form.

A general rejection of Marx's theory on the grounds that he did not consider certain species of commodity exchange and of capital does not withstand scrutiny. The various species mentioned by Winfield are all explicitly acknowledged in *Capital*. And there are good reasons for thinking that these species do not all fall on the same level from a systematic perspective.

The final area I would like to explore also involves a genus-species relation. It concerns both the central substantive argument in Winfield's book and the most important divergence between Hegel and Marx. The argument may be put as follows:

> 1. The just economy is characterized by civil freedom; that is, "each participant [acts] in view of his own interest in cooperation with others insofar as his aim [can] only be achieved by simultaneously honoring their concordant exercise of that same freedom. Such an arrangement [allows] for a just community of interest in which the free realization of each member's personal ends figures as a right that all are duty-bound to respect insofar as only in so doing can they engage in their own respected pursuit of interest."[28]
> 2. Civil freedom demands that individual economic agents are at liberty to develop their conventional needs, to choose the means for satisfying these needs, and to select the form of employment that provides access to these means, subject only to the constraint that these decisions must be compatible with those made by other, equally free, economic agents.
> 3. An economy based on commodity exchange is the only species of economy in which civil freedom can be institutionalized.
> 4. Therefore, the only just economy is one based on commodity exchange.

For Winfield there is no greater example of Hegel's abiding importance for social philosophy than the fact that he was the first to present this argument in an adequate fashion. And there is no greater example of Marx's failure as a social thinker than his failure to accept this Hegelian perspective.

The first and second premises can be granted. The third premise, however needs to be scrutinized. In a Marxist reading of Hegel the third premise must be considerably weakened. The Marxist view is that whatever his intentions Hegel merely provided a defense for a species of economy that best allowed civil freedom in a past epoch. In contrast, Winfield believed that Hegel made a warranted transcendental claim: commodity relations universally and necessarily define the only species of economy that counts as just: "Only within a market, a context where a plurality of commodity owners can freely enter into exchange, can need enjoy the legitimacy of being the particular end pursued within the reciprocal relation of civil freedom."

To justify such a strong claim Winfield needed to dismiss not just every alternative economic system that ever existed, but every other logically possible species of economy: "Other economic arrangements may be topics of descriptive analysis, but [commodity exchange] alone offers a field for developing an independent economic justice."[29]

Winfield argued for the plausibility of this through a consideration of the economic system he regarded as the most attractive alternative to a commodity exchange economy. This is a democratically planned economy in which every economic agent has an equal voice in the determination of the plan. In his view the fundamental flaw in this model lies in the fact that the plan ultimately is decided through majority vote. This means that all those in the minority would have their conventional needs, the means to satisfy those needs, and their mode of employment imposed on them. Hence, even a democratically planned economy does not meet the condition for being a just economy:

> Such a "democratization" may give each participant an equal say in managing the economy of the community, but it does so only by taking away their personal freedom to select their own occupation or the goods they want. By "democratizing" their economy and making the will of the majority the unique arbiter of vocation and need, individuals relinquish their autonomy of interest in both regards.[30]

Two comments are in order. First, we should note that free consent to a decision procedure implies free consent to the results attained by that procedure, even if one disagrees with the results in a particular case. I strongly suspect that Winfield would not say that in a political democracy citizens lose their political freedom whenever they find themselves in a minority. Why should we assert that economic agents within economic democracy necessarily would lose their civil freedom whenever they found themselves in the minority? If these agents freely agreed that the procedure of democratic planning was superior to other procedures,[31] then they would freely consent to the results attained by that procedure, even if in a particular case they would have preferred a different outcome. (We should also remember that markets also continually leave considerable numbers of people unhappy with their outcome. Winfield admitted this, yet nowhere suggested that this undermines the civil freedom of these people).

Second, Winfield presupposed that economic plans must be formulated in a manner that takes no account of the preferences of individuals regarding their needs, the manner of satisfying these needs, and their place of employment. There does not seem to be any valid reason for holding this supposition. Imagine a society that combined a commitment to socialism with the latest advances in communications technology. At the beginning of a production period[32] all economic agents punch their consumption requests into a terminal, along with their preferences regarding place of employment. If the allocation of the labor force into different sectors exactly corresponds to the proportions in which consumption items were requested, then all is well and good. If not, adjustments would have to be made. Information regarding the imbalances in the economy could be transmitted back to the economic agents, who are thus encouraged to modify their consumption requests and employment preferences accordingly. This would bring the plan closer to an efficient matching of supply with articulated social needs. If imbalances remain at the end of this procedure, only then would alternative plans for resolving them be submitted to democratic discussion and vote.

Of course, this is a very simplified sketch. But it is detailed enough to show that, although the free choices of economic agents are constrained, they are constrained only by the free choices of other economic agents. In other words, this economy would institutionalize civil freedom as defined by Winfield himself.

The species of economy has never existed, nor is it on the historical agenda today. And I have not offered any argument suggesting that it could function efficiently in comparison to commodity exchange economies. The only point I have been trying to make is that such an economy is logically possible. If this is granted, then the transcendental claim first affirmed by Hegel and subsequently repeated by Winfield cannot be defended. It is mistaken to argue that a commodity exchange economy in principle is the only just economy. The species of economy sketched here is based on free and reciprocal agreements and yet does not involve the production and distribution of commodities.

Winfield's book allows us to grasp both some of the main features of Hegelian social theory and a number of significant Hegelian objections to Marxist theory. It is now time to turn from debates within the tradition of dialectical social theory to criticism of this tradition.

PART TWO

CONTEMPORARY CRITICISMS OF DIALECTICAL SOCIAL THEORY

V

Hegelianism and Marx: A Reply to Lucio Colletti

In the preface to *Socialism: Utopian and Scientific* Engels wrote that, "We Germans are proud of the fact that we are descendants not only of Saint-Simon, Fourier and Owen, but also of Kant, Fichte and Hegel."[1] It has been widely accepted by the students of Marx that of the latter group Hegel made the greatest contribution to Marxism. Lucio Colletti's *Marxism and Hegel*[2] provides a vehement attack on this perspective. In Colletti's view, Hegelianism is antithetical to Marx's standpoint on most essential points. He argued that Marx's true philosophical predecessor is Kant, not Hegel, and that the influence of Hegel on those following Marx has been pernicious. Despite the massive rethinking of the historical roots of Marxism this thesis requires, Colletti's interpretation already has proven quite influential.[3] This chapter is an attempt to consider whether Colletti's view of the relation between Marx and Hegel is justified.

In the first section Colletti's main arguments are presented. In the second section these arguments are subjected to criticism, building on Part One of this book. I will show that despite an impressive appearance of scholarship Colletti seriously misunderstands central features of both Hegel's system and the logical framework of Marx's theory. When these mistakes are corrected, it becomes clear that Hegel's importance for Marx's thought has been seriously underestimated. This, however, does not mean that the positions of Marx and Hegel are to be conflated. In the previous chapter we saw how the analysis of generalized commodity exchange provided by the two thinkers differed. In the conclusion to his chapter the manner in which Marx can be said to have defended a "materialist" position against Hegel's "idealism" will be briefly presented.

Colletti on Hegel, Kant, and Marx's Epigone

For Colletti, Hegel's thought represented a return to pre-Kantian metaphysics, a metaphysics by and large embodying principles of Christianity. Two closely related theses lie at the heart of this metaphysics: the priority of the ideal over the material, and the eradication of the independent existence of individual finite entities. Colletti often discussed Hegel's alleged eradication of the material interchangeably with his alleged eradication of the finite. But the two points are distinct in principle. It is certainly possible to conceive of one without the other, say, a philosophical defense of idealism in which ideal but finite objects retained their independent existence. Accordingly, each thesis will be discussed in turn.

Hegel's Alleged Eradication of the Material

Hegel distinguished two processes. The first is the "process of reality" or the "natural process," the second the "logical process" or the "logicodeductive process." In the former the empirical realm is prior, placing limiting conditions on thought. In the latter, Colletti wrote:

> Thought *cancels* out – dialecticizing them – the limiting conditions or premises in reality upon which it appeared to depend... it transforms the empirical being on which it appeared to depend into one of its own effects or consequences.... In the process of development "according to nature," the Notion comes second and reality first. In the logical process, it is the other way round, the Notion first and reality second; that is to say, reality is deduced and derived from the Notion.[4]

It is not the distinction of these two processes *per se* that distinguishes Hegel's philosophy. Colletti asserted that in "any other genuine thought" the distinction is to be found as well.[5] What is unique to Hegel in Colletti's reading is the utter failure to attain a proper balance between the two processes. The second process swallows the first. The independent reality of the first process is an illusion; it is merely an appearance of the logical process, which is prior, independent, and self-generating: "Hegel's solution was to downgrade the process of development 'according to nature' into an *apparent* process. The process of development 'according to the notion,' on the other hand, is upgraded into a *real* process. In other words, the process in reality or according to nature is reduced to an 'appearance' or manifestation of the logical process, the process according to the notion."[6] With this move the independence of the material realm has been eradicated:

> "Real" are not those things external to thought, but those things penetrated by thought ("pensate"): i.e. those things which are *no longer things* but simple "logical objects" or ideal moments. The negation, the "annihilation" of matter is precisely in this passage from "outside" to "within."[7]

> By declaring matter "essential" only as it is in thought, it is *ipso facto* excluded that the former has any reality as it is outside and antecedent to the Notion.[8]

This, for Colletti, is all in the starkest contrast to the materialism of Marx. Marx too begins by distinguishing the natural process from the logical process of theory building. But Marx rejected Hegel's idealistic supersession of the objective and material. In Marx's thought the two processes are kept in a balance in which the materialist moment is irreducible to thought: "Like every genuine thinker, Marx recognizes the irreplaceable role of the logicodeductive process. . . . But, as opposed to Hegel, Marx upholds the process of reality side-by-side with the logical process. The passage from the abstract to the concrete is only the way in which thought appropriates reality; it is not to be confused with the way in which the concrete itself originates."[9]

Hegel's Alleged Eradication of the Finite

In Colletti's interpretation, for Hegel the intellect is that faculty which interprets the world in terms of finite individual things. It does so through employing the principles of identity and noncontradiction, by means of which each finite thing maintains its uniqueness in distinction from every other finite entity. At the heart of Hegel's philosophy, Colletti argued, lies the view that this perspective is mistaken. Colletti quoted Hegel's dictum that "the finite has no veritable being,"[10] and concluded that, for Hegel,

> The finite is that which is fated to come to an end: that which is evanescent and devoid of value. . . . If in fact the principle of philosophy is that the finite is *non-being* and only the infinite *is*, philosophy can lay claim to logical consistency in its operations only under one condition: that it puts an end to the finite and validates only the infinite, thereby annihilating the world and replacing it with "true" reality."[11]

To affirm this is to abandon the intellect and its principle of noncontradiction: "In the process of dissolving things and the entire finite world, it annihilates, by that very act, the determination of the 'intellect,' or in other words, all those determinate propositions and statements founded on the principle of non-contradiction, to which thought remains bound as long as it considers itself tied to and constricted by the existence of factual data."[12] It is to affirm that the finite "passes over" to its underlying essence, an essence that remains after it, the finite, has ceased to be.[13] This essence, the "infinite," alone truly is.

This does not mean that an individual finite thing has no ontological status whatsoever. It is an appearance (*Schein*) of the underlying essence:

> In order to comprehend the infinite in a coherent fashion, the finite must be destroyed, the world annihilated: the infinite, in fact, cannot have alongside itself another reality which limits it. On the other hand, once the finite is expunged and that which thrust the infinite into the *beyond* — making it an "empty ideal," devoid of real existence — is suppressed, the infinite can pass over from the beyond to the *here and now*, that is, become flesh and take on earthly attire.[14]

As this passage suggests, for Colletti Hegel's style was merely a variant of traditional Judeo-Christian metaphysics,[15] a variant anticipated by Spinoza's similar eradication of the independence of finite entities.[16]

In Colletti's view all this is in stark contrast to Marx's viewpoint. For Hegel the ideal, the universal, stands over and above finite individuals so that the latter ultimately have no independent ontological status. But for Marx the universal lacks ontological substantiality; only finite individuals exist as subjects. Any attempt to set up a reified universal existing above finite individuals reduces true subjects (the individuals) to mere predicates of an illusionary subject (the universal).[17] "For Marx, in fact, metaphysics is the *realism of universals*. It is a logical totality which posits itself as self-subsisting, transforms itself into the subject, and which (since it must be self-subsisting) identifies and confuses itself acritically with the particular, turning the latter — i.e. the actual subject of reality — into its own predicate or manifestation."[18] Insofar as Marx wished to oppose a science of political economy to Hegelian metaphysics, the principle of identity and noncontradiction must be recovered, for this principle is the foundation for all empirical science. And this recovery is carried through precisely by overcoming the reification of universals (the elimination of the finite) on which Hegel's system is built.[19]

Colletti, of course, did not deny that Hegel made a number of profound contributions to the development of Marx's thought. Hegel, after all, first realized the centrality of labor in human history.[20] Nevertheless, in questions of epistemology and ontology Marx's great predecessor according to Colletti was Kant, not Hegel. For in Kant we find a clear affirmation that existence is not a predicate, that being cannot be reduced to a mere logical category, that it is "something more" than thought.[21]

From this perspective the history of "Marxist" thought has been one of continued divergence from Marx's own position. For in Colletti's view the two major branches of Marxist philosophy — orthodox dialectical materialism (going back to Engels and Lenin) and Western Marxism (including thinkers such as the early Lukács and the members of the Frankfurt School) — *both* involve a return to Hegelian themes unequivocally rejected by Marx himself. The dialectical materialism of orthodox Marxism accepts Hegel's abandonment of the principle of noncontradiction. It thereby replaces Marx's own concern for empirical science with a speculative philosophy of nature *a la* Hegel. In doing so it conflates real conflict with logical opposition and loses the "something more" that separates being from thought.[22] Western Marxism, although rejecting any theory of a dialectic of matter, makes a similar error. Its adherence to Hegelian dialectics leads it to formulate a critique of the principles of identity and noncontradiction employed by empirical sciences, which it then confuses with a critique of capitalism.[23] As a result, "The difference between 'dialectical materialism' and 'Western Marxism' shows itself in a novel light; i.e., not so much as a difference between Marxism of a materialist cast and Marxism *qua* 'philosophy of praxis,' but rather as the difference between two opposing and greatly adulterated offshoots of the same Hegelian tradition.[24] Colletti concludes that Marxism will be able to present an adequate philosophical position only if it overcomes its infatuation with Hegel and returns to the materialiam of Marx himself, a materialism anticipated in the work of Kant.

Hegel and the Hegelianism of Marx

In the remainder of this chapter I attempt to evaluate Colletti's reading of Hegel and the relationship between Hegel and Marx. If, as I argue, Colletti was seriously mistaken here, then his position on Kant, orthodox Marxism, and Western Marxism would have to be rethought as well. This, however, will not be attempted here. Earlier Colletti's critique of Hegel was divided into two sections. This division will be retained.

The Materialist Moment in Hegel

In the conclusion to this chapter I will show how and why it indeed is proper to contrast Hegel's "idealism" with Marx's "materialism." But I do not believe it is proper to locate this contrast where Colletti did, in the manner in which the two combine the process according to nature (the empirical process) with the process according to thought (the logicodeductive process). Colletti's thesis was that Hegel reduced the former to the latter whereas Marx did not. In my response the main stages in the methodology of Hegel and Marx will be recalled (the first three subsections).[25] I then argue that both Hegel and Marx held that the process of thought is independent from the real process (the fourth subsection); that Hegel, no less than Marx, held that the real process is autonomous from the thought process in at least four different respects (the fifth subsection); and that Marx, no less than Hegel, granted the thought process priority over the real process (the final subsection). It follows that this aspect of Colletti's Hegel critique does not withstand scrutiny. Let us begin with the three stages of dialectical methodology.

The Starting Point

In Marx's methodological reflections the starting point for theory building is the real process, "the real and concrete" as given in experience.[26] But as immediately experienced it is not possible to have more than a "chaotic conception of the whole" of this experience. Hence there is a need to proceed to the theorizing of that experience. For Hegel, "philosophy is its own time apprehended in thoughts. It is just as absurd to fancy that a philosophy can transcend its contemporary world as it is to fancy that an individual can overleap his own age."[27] This means that for Hegel too the point of departure is the immediately given experience at a particular historical juncture. But here too the immediate experience is "chaotic" or, in Hegel's words, not "apprehended." And so here too thought proceeds from the initially given onward.

The Analytic-Regressive Stage

One type of theorizing, found in what we may call the positivist sciences, sticks close to the initially given appearances and proposes various concepts to grasp these appearances. These concepts for the most part are thrown out haphazardly and fall on many different levels of generality. Such, at least, was the case with respect to the concepts of political economy proposed prior to Marx. The second stage of Marx's method is to begin an analysis of the uncomprehended experience through an appropriation of these concepts. But this appropriation is not haphazard; already a systematic intention is at work. This intention is expressed in working through concepts with the goal of reaching those that are simplest and most abstract (such as "commodity," "use value," "exchange value," etc. in *Capital*). From "a chaotic conception of the whole," Marx wrote, "I would then, by means of further determination, move analytically towards ever more simple concepts, from the imagined concrete towards ever thinner abstractions until I had arrived at the simplest determinations."[28]

Hegel too proceeded to an analysis of uncomprehended experience through an appropriation of the empirical concepts proposed in the positivist sciences. This empiricist moment in Hegel's methodology often is overlooked, but it is clearly stated in passages such as the following: "The knowledge of the particular is necessary. This particularity must be worked out on its own account; we must become acquainted with empirical nature, both with the physical and with the human.... Without the working out of the empirical sciences on their own account, Philosophy could not have reached further than with the ancients."[29] And for Hegel too this appropriation has the systematic intention of arriving at the simplest and most abstract determinations of thought (e.g., "being" in the *Logic*, "property" in the *Philosophy of Right*, etc.).[30]

The Synthetic-Progressive Stage

Having arrived at the "simplest determinations," Marx continued as follows: "From there the journey would have to be retraced until I had finally arrived at the [concrete], but this time not as the chaotic conception of a whole, but as a rich totality of many determinations and relations."[31] This involves a systematic reconstruction of the categories appropriated in the second stage (supplemented where necessary), a progression from the most simple and concrete determinations to the most complex and concrete ones. At the end, the intelligibility of the initially given concrete will have been grasped by thought in a systematic fashion.

> The concrete is concrete because it is the concentration of many determinations hence unity of the diverse. It appears in the process of thinking, therefore, as a process of concentration, as a result, not as a point of departure, even though it is the point of departure in reality and hence also the point of departure for observation and conception. Along the first path the full conception was evaporated to yield an abstract determination; along the second, the abstract determinations lead towards a reproduction of the concrete by way of thought.[32]

This is precisely the architectonic of Hegel's system as well. His system consists of a linear progression of categories likewise ordered from the simple and abstract to the complex and concrete. (I shall have more to say about this architectonic later.)

This completes the summary of the stages of the thought process. Next the mediation between it and the real process must be examined.

The Independence of the Thought Process

This point follows directly from the preceding. Hegel's insistence on the independence of the thought process is certainly beyond doubt and does not need to be established in detail here. For him, the systematic progression of categories follows an immanent logical ordering distinct from the order of events in immediate experience: "What we acquire...is a series of thoughts and another series of existent shapes of experience; to which I may add that the time order in which the latter actually appear is other than the logical order. Thus, for example, we cannot say that property *existed* before the family, yet, in spite of that, property must be dealt with first."[33]

The assertion that Marx too granted an independence to the thought process is more controversial. It is certainly true that Marx's references to real historical processes in *Capital* (the primative accumulation of capital in England, the intertwining of the history of class struggle and that of technology, etc.) go far beyond anything to be found in Hegel. Hegel's historical references are mostly digressions from his systematic ordering of categories. These comments are found for the most part not in the text itself, but rather in notes taken from Hegel's lectures and added to the text under the heading "Additions." In contrast, the method Marx employs in *Capital* is a "structural-genetic" method in which systematic considerations of the logical progression of thought are indissolvably mixed with historical considerations.[34] Nonetheless, Marx insisted that the process of thought does not merely echo the unfolding of the real process: "It would be unfeasible and wrong to let the economic categories follow one another in the same sequence as that in which they were historically decisive."[35] The model presented at the beginning of *Capital*, for example, does not represent some stage of simple commodity production historically prior to industrial capitalism.[36] No such stage has existed in history. The categories at the beginning of *Capital* instead are thought constructs won by abstracting from the capitalist mode of production all but its simplest elements. Marx, proceeding systematically to progressively more advanced categories, then reconstructed the inner logic of this mode of production. This systematic ordering follows its own immanent progression, from "value" through "money," "production of capital," and "circulation of capital," to "distribution of capital," to name the most important stages in the process from simple and abstract determinations to complex and concrete categories. As already insisted on in Chapter III, this ordering obviously is distinct from that whereby one phase of history replaces another. Therefore the process of thought is independent of the historical process no less in Marx than in Hegel.

The Autonomy of the Real Process in Hegel

Does Hegel's granting of independence to the process of thought commit him to an eradication of the real material process? No. Hegel no more does this than Marx, who as we have just seen also granted an independence to the thought process.

In asserting that Hegel ultimately denied the autonomy of the real process Colletti simply repeated Marx's claim that

> Hegel fell into the illusion of conceiving the real as a product of thought concentrating itself, probing its own depths, and unfolding itself out of itself, by itself, whereas the method of rising from the abstract to the concrete is only the way in which thought appropriates the concrete, reproduces it as the concrete in the mind. But this is by no means the process by which the concrete itself comes into being.[37]

Both Colletti and Marx were wrong here. The following are just some of the ways in which the real material process retains its independence from the process of thought in Hegel.

First, as we have seen in our discussion of what was termed the *analytic-regressive stage*, the process of thought does not spring out of thin air. It is dependent on the material process in that the systematic ordering of categories is a reconstruction of categories initially won in confrontation with the empirically given. As if in anticipation of Marx's criticism that in his methodology "thought unfolds itself out of itself, by itself," Hegel wrote

> In order that this science [i.e., Hegel's system] may come into existence, we must have the progression from the individual and particular to the universal — an activity which is a reaction on the given material of empiricism in order to bring about its reconstruction. The demand of *a priori* knowledge, which seems to imply that the idea should construct from itself, is thus a reconstruction only.... In consciousness it then adopts the attitude of having cut away the bridge from behind it; it appears to be free to launch forth in its ether only, and to develop without resistance to this medium; but it is another matter to attain to this ether and to development of it.[38]

Second, in the subsection "The Independence of the Thought Process" I showed that the ordering of categories proposed in the process of thought does not follow the ordering of empirical events. The converse, of course, holds as well: this historical progression in the real process is not reducible to the logical progression of categories within Hegel's system. For example, were the real material process reducible to a mere appearance of the logical process, as Colletti and Marx presupposed it is in Hegel, then it would seem to follow that from grasp of the latter one could extrapolate to the course future events must follow with logical necessity. But Hegel made no such move. He instead acknowledged that the real process has its own pattern of future development, one irreducible to the pattern of logical development in the process of thought.[39]

Third, in Hegel, the independence of the materially given from thought is not merely a function of its following a distinct ordering. For Hegel — no less than for Kant or Marx — there remains a "something other" that separates the material from thought. In the real process there is an irreducible residue of contingency, a surd without an intelligibility to be grasped by thought, an element that cannot be reduced to logical categories. Hegel acknowledged this residue of the material impenetrable by thought at practically every stage of his system. It is found, to list just some examples, in the individual soul,[40] in the content of sensations,[41] in the workings of the market place,[42] in the content of positive laws,[43] and in history.[44] At points such as these thought confronts the "something other" than itself. Because Hegel acknowledged a contingency and accidentality in the real process that cannot be reduced to categories, he does not reduce the material world to logical necessity. Its independence is guaranteed.

Fourth, as we saw earlier in the discussion of the starting point of theory, for Hegel, philosophy is "its time apprehended in thoughts." The real process, the process of history, asserts its independence from the thought process by providing the ultimate horizon within which the thought process is situated. Could there be any doubt, for example, that a "Hegelian" system constructed in Classical Greece or Medieval Europe would be radically different from what Hegel himself constructed in nineteeth century Germany? Classical Greece, Hegel would point out, lacked the principle of subjectivity. Medieval Europe had that principle, but had no way of reconciling it with an Essence that it conceived as lying "Beyond." Any reconstruction of categories during those periods would differ drastically from Hegel's in which — Hegel would insist — these problems had been overcome. Also, I already have noted that in Hegel's view philosophy cannot fully develop prior to the historical rise of the empirical sciences. These points show that the thought systems constructed in the history of philosophy cannot go beyond the level attained in a particular period of historical development. They are instead dependent on the principles attained by their historical period. Thus the former (the logical process) does not at all negate the independence of the latter (the real process).

The Priority of the Thought Process in Marx

Hegel did not negate the independence of the material any more than did Marx. The final point to be made here is that Marx did not grant any less of a priority to the thought process than did Hegel.

Colletti's insistence on the priority of the real process and empirical science in Marx sounds at first hearing convincing and materialist. But if Marx had adhered to Colletti's position, *Capital* would never have been written and historical materialism would never have arisen. For as we saw in Chapter III it is a central thesis of Marx's position that in capitalism the real process necessarily generates appearances that are illusionary. Those immersed within the real process inevitably consider "price" and "supply and demand" fundamental economic categories, see the wage contract as a free exchange of equivalents, see "capital" as a productive factor in its own right, and so on. Empirical sciences that do not call into question the priority of the real process make such appearances the first principles of their theories. The result is what Marx termed *vulgar economics*, not historical materialism. *The intelligibility of the concrete and material can be grasped only through asserting the priority of the thought process over how the concrete and material is given in appearances.* For the concrete and material has a depth level of essence underlying its surface level of appearances. The task of thought is first to pierce through the appearances to that depth level (the level of "value" as measured by labor-time rather than "price," where exploitation is discovered within the wage contract, where only labor counts as productive of value, and so on) and then to proceed to the mediations that connect the level of essence with that of appearances. To fulfill this task it is not sufficient for thought to assert its independence; it must assert its primacy over the real process and the appearances it generates. Here too there is no difference in principle between Marx and Hegel.

We have examined the different stages in the process of thought as articulated in the methodologies of Hegel and Marx. We also have discussed the mediations between the thought process and the real process. It has been shown that Hegel did not eradicate the material realm by reducing the real process to the process of thought, nor did he grant the process of thought any sort of priority not also granted by Marx. The difference between the two thinkers does not lie here, contrary to Colletti's interpretation. It is true that Hegel stressed the logical necessity that he felt characterizes the ordering of categories constituting his system. It is also true that Marx stressed the independence of the material realm from thought. But each thinker's position also embodies the point stressed by the other. Hegel thematized the "otherness" of the material, and Marx's theory too includes logical necessity (for instance, the category "value" precedes with logical necessity the category "price" in

Marx's reconstruction of the system of categories grasping the capitalist mode of production). Colletti, therefore, was wrong to contrast Marx's "materialism" to Hegel's "idealism" based on how the real process is related to the thought process in their work.

The Importance of the Finite Individual in Hegel

In addition to Hegel's supposed eradication of the material, Colletti presented a second set of reasons why Hegel's thought is antithetical to that of Marx. Hegel rejected the principle of identity and noncontradiction and he reified universals. He therefore negated the independent existence of the finite, the individual. Here too I argue that Colletti's interpretation was mistaken. There is no difference between Hegel and Marx here, on the level of philosophical principles. The differences between the two theorists, to which we shall return in the conclusion, arise in the process of applying these principles to the empirical realm. Four topics will be discussed in the reply to Colletti: the status of the principle of noncontradiction in Hegel, the question of the reification of universals, the move from "essence" (*Wesen*) to "the notion" (*Begriff*) in Hegel's system, and the nature of the finite in Marx.

The Principle of Identity and Noncontradiction in Hegel

A first argument supporting Colletti's claim that Hegel eliminates the finite can be summarized as follows. The retention of the finite demands that one finite thing be kept distinct from another in our thought; the principle of identity and noncontradiction is necessary to accomplish this; Hegel abandoned that principle in his dialectical logic; therefore Hegel eradicated the finite.

This argument fails to take into account the fact that earlier stages in Hegel's system are not simply abandoned as the system proceeds. They instead are retained, but retained as subordinate moments with only a relative right.[45] When this is brought into play, Colletti's criticism loses its force. The principle of noncontradiction has a place in Hegel's system.[46] And it retained its relative right when Hegel proceeded to further categories.

The best way to grasp how Hegel retained the principle of identity and noncontradiction (and therefore the moment of the finite individual) is by reconstructing why Hegel went beyond this principle. Consider a heap of universal things randomly thrown together. Each is different from the others in a way made intelligible by the principle in question. Now consider the parts of a living organic whole, for instance the different organs of the body. These parts also are distinct from each other; the heart is not the liver. And so the principle of identity and noncontradiction retains validity here too. But now we are no longer dealing with an aggregate of unrelated entities or, rather, with entities in merely external relations to each other. The heart and the liver are united together in the organism even while remaining distinct. To thematize this, Hegel introduced categories capable of going beyond the fixity of "identity" and "difference," categories that allow us to speak of a "unity-in-difference." Dialectical logic, which would talk of the organism as a unity of identity (the organism as a whole) and difference (the different parts that make up the organism) thus "goes beyond" the principle of identity and noncontradiction. The latter can be used to formulate the differences of a part from other parts, whereas the former can grasp this *as well as* the union of these different parts within the whole. But dialectical logic does not reject the principle of identity and noncontradiction. The same thing is not both affirmed and denied of the same object at the same time in the same respect. Dialectical logic does not make the heart into the liver! Colletti's first argument for accusing Hegel of negating the finite thus misses the mark: finite things can be distinguished even while affirming a logic of unity-in-difference that goes beyond the principle of identity and noncontradiction.

The Question of the Reification of Universals in Hegel

A second agrument proposed by Colletti can be given the following formulation. Finite individuals are real subjects. Hegel's reification of universals reduces these real subjects to mere predicates of an imaginary subject, the universal. Therefore Hegel's recourse to universals does not allow room for finite individuals in his system.

This objection, although true to Marx's criticism of Hegel, entirely misses the ontological status of universals in Hegel's thought. Throughout the history of metaphysics a battle has raged. On one side stand those who grant universals an independent reality ("realists"). On the other are those who insist that only individuals are "really real" and that universals are mere names ("nominalists"). From Hegel's perspective, both of these views are one-sided and nondialectical. Nominalists are not content with a dumb staring at the individual things of sense perception. They wish to know these things, presupposing thereby that individual things are intelligible. The knowledge, this capturing of the intelligibility of individual things, can be won only through employing universals. To not grant these universals independent ontological status therefore would be to deny both the possibility of knowledge and the intelligibility of individual things, and thus to contradict the nominalists' own activity.[47] Likewise universals are merely empty concepts without objective import when they are not connected with existing individual things. Thus Hegel concluded that *both* universals and individuals must be acknowledged in any adequate ontology. Neither can be accepted consistently without also accepting the other; without universals individual things would have no intelligibility, and without individual things universals would have no existential import. Only the two together capture the whole.[48]

The aim here is not to defend Hegel's ontology. The point to be established is simply that it was possible for Hegel to grant universals an ontological status *without* reifying them; that is, without asserting that they are "real subjects" claiming existing individuals as their predicates. From this we can fix more precisely the ontological status to be assigned universals within Hegel's system. In his view a universal is a unifying principle of thought that grasps the intelligibility of individual things. In contrast, "real subjects" are what are brought into a unity and principled.

We can illustrate this point best with references to the part of Hegel's system most often pointed out as an example of a reification of universals, his theory of the state. Both Marx and Colletti accused Hegel of having made the state, a universal, into the real subject of the political process, thereby reducing individual citizens to being mere predicates of it. But for Hegel the state *qua* universal is *not* a "real" entity. It is rather an intelligible principle whereby real entities are united. Specifically, Hegel defined the state in terms of "the spirit of a people"[49] or "the spirit of a nation."[50] This is a *principle* and not a *thing*, although Hegel is quick to assert that such principles have an ontological status no less than the things principled. The "real subjects" remain the individual citizens of the state, who are united into a political community through that principle. Consider Hegel's definition of the state: "The state... is the actuality of the substantial will *which it possesses in the particular self-consciousness* once that consciousness has been raised to consciousness of its universality."[51] The substantial will that is the basis of the state is the principle unifying the political community. It is a universal. It is granted an ontological status distinct from the particular self-consciousness of individual citizens. It is even said by Hegel in the following sentences to be "an absolute end in itself" with "supreme right against the individual, whose supreme duty is to be a member of the state" (more on this later). But the substantial will is *not* said to be the real subject in which the particular self-consciousness of individual citizens inheres as a mere predicate. On the contrary, the substantial will, the universal, is said to have real existence ("actuality") in the particular self-consciousness of individual citizens.[52] *Contra* Colletti, I conclude that granting ontological status to a unifying principle does not in itself commit Hegel to a negation of the finite individual things unified together by that principle.[53]

The Transition from Essence to the Notion in Hegel

It has just been established that Hegel's use of universals does not in itself automatically lead to the eradication of the finite individual. But Hegel still may have reached that result nonetheless, depending on the precise manner in which universal and individual are mediated in his system. Colletti's case here rests on a great number of passages in which Hegel clearly appears to dissolve the finite into the universal.

Before considering this objection, it is important to note first that assertions made by Hegel must be clearly situated within the architectonic of Hegel's system if they are to be properly understood. For the passages quoted by Colletti in which Hegel appears to dissolve the finite either come from a specific place in Hegel's system or directly refer to what is established at that place. To understand why this is significant we must briefly attempt to sketch the main divisions of Hegel's *Logic*.

The *Logic* is divided into three subdivisions. In the first section, Being (*Sein*), categories are presented that constitute a one-tiered ontology, an ontology of individual things in external relations. Hegel attempted to show that this is an impoverished ontology. This led him to the second subdivision, Essence (*Wesen*). Here categories making up a two-tiered ontology are presented, with the level of individual things now subsumed under and reduced to a level that is their "ground" or "essence." In the final section, the Notion (*Begriff*), Hegel introduced categories that allow for a mediation between these two levels, a unity-in-difference in which each pole remains distinct from the other while being united with it in a structured totality. Now every passage quoted by Colletti on Hegel's "dissolution of the finite" comes from the first two parts of the system or refers back to points established there. On the level of Being, the lack of independence of finite individuals is precisely what must be stressed to motivate the introduction of an "essence" underlying them. And on the level of Essence this same point is considered to think through a two-tiered ontology that avoids proclaiming appearances the sole reality. But on the ultimate level, that of the Notion, it is stressed that the universal, the whole, the essence, the infinite, cannot be thought coherently on its own apart from the particular, the part, the appearances, the finite, any more than the reverse can be done. A central task here is to derive categories that preserve the moment of difference, the autonomy of finite individuals within the whole.

Let us now consider two typical statements by Colletti:

> 'Being which is *per se* straightway non-being we call a show, a semblance (*Schein*)'. (Hegel) And if the finite, the particular, does not have being in itself, but has as its 'essence' or 'foundation' the 'other', it is clear that, in order to be itself, the finite has to 'pass over' into the infinite, cancel itself out.[54]

> Once the finite's 'illusory' independence has been negated, once it has been recognized that the finite does not have being in and of itself, that it is only 'illusory being' (*Schein*), and that 'its' essence lies beyond itself, the finite becomes exactly the illusory being or *appearance* of that essence, the *beyond* of that beyond.[55]

Even the extremely elementary summary of Hegel's architectonic just given allows us to see that Colletti has not grasped Hegel's final word on the issue. The categories "show," "semblance," "essence," "appearance," etc. are *all* categories assigned by Hegel to the level of Essence. They therefore have only qualified and relative validity. On the level of the Notion, the finite is *not* a mere appearance of Essence. *That stage has been unequivocally left behind*. Here the finite individual retains its autonomy and distinctness in the fullest fashion, while at the same time retaining its innermost substantial unity with the universal. To assert, for example, that only within a community can the individual self flourish is not at all to negate that individual self. Just the opposite. This was Hegel's position. Armed with these categories from the level of Notion, he employed the full autonomy of the finite individual in the sociopolitical realm as a criterion to judge both the legitimacy of the state and progress in history.[56]

To reduce Hegel's ontology to a "tautoheterology" in which the difference of the individual and finite from the universal is a difference that makes no difference is equivalent to thinking Hegel concluded his system of categories with the level of Essence. It is to reduce Hegel to a nineteenth century Spinoza, reducing finite individuality to a mere mode or attribute of Substance, when the stress on the autonomy of the finite individual is precisely what *distinguishes* Hegel from Spinoza.[57] It is, in brief, to not comprehend Hegel.

Colletti's thesis was that Hegel's philosophical framework involves an eradication of the finite totally incompatible with Marx's thought. Three central features of Hegel's philosophical framework have been examined: the use of a logic going beyond the principle of identity and noncontradiction, the introduction of universals, and the specific manner in which Hegel mediates the relations between the universal and the individual. It has been shown that none of these features implies a negation of the finite individual. On the contrary, at the culmination of Hegel's system the idea that the finite individual is a mere appearance of an essence standing above it is explicitly *rejected*. The independence of the finite individual instead is insisted on. One final point remains to be established before the reply to Colletti will be completed. It must be shown that within Marx's philosophical framework the individual has exactly the same ontological status as in Hegel.

Marx and the Finite

Central to Marx's philosophical framework is a mode of analysis that goes beyond the principle of identity and noncontradiction, stresses the importance of universals, and thematizes the mediation between the universal and the finite individual in a manner identical with Hegel's move from essence to the notion. Because he shared these features with Hegel, Marx "negated" the finite no less — and no more — than Hegel.[58] This can be shown with respect to both Marx's analysis of capitalism and his projection of a future society based on council democracy.

We can begin with a simplified presentation of Marx's model of the capitalist mode of production. Marx's analysis examines the circuit of capital, its metamorphosis. This circuit can be diagramed as follows:

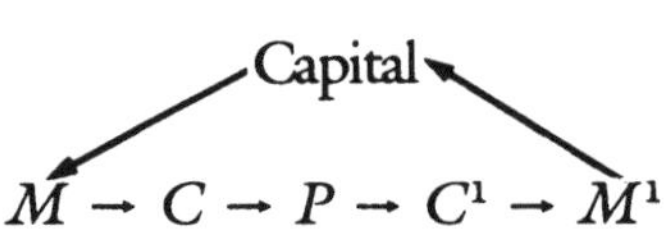

Capital first takes on the form of money capital (M). This money capital is then invested in the purchase of certain commodities (C), specifically, means of production and labor power. Next comes the production process (P), in which labor power is set to work on the means of production. At its conclusion a new commodity (C^1) has been produced; capital takes on the form of inventory capital. Finally, we move from the process of production back to the process of circulation with selling the product. If the product is successfully sold for a profit, so that $M^1 > M$, capital takes on a form adequate to its essence: money has begot money. Some of this fund is then devoted to capitalist consumption. The remainder is accumulated and reinvested, beginning the circuit anew.

In analyzing the inner logic of this circuit, the principle of identity and noncontradiction holds. The different individual forms of capital remain distinct from each other; for example, the production of capital is not the circulation of capital. But Marx's analysis goes beyond a mere assertion of these differences. The intelligibility of the process cannot be grasped without seeing that these stages are united at the same time that they are distinct. The formal principle of identity and noncontradiction therefore must be supplemented with the dialectical principle of unity-in-difference. Marx's theory of economic crisis rests on this point. Within the capitalist mode of production it is possible for one form of capital to set itself off as independent from the sale of commodities. This, however, creates the possibility that the whole circuit will collapse in crisis. The course of this crisis consists in the assertion of a unity that "negates" the claim to independence on the part of the finite forms just as forcefully as any "negation" of the finite in Hegel: "*Crisis* is nothing but the forcible assertion of the unity of phases of the production process which have become independent of each other."[59] Marx clearly employed Hegel's dialectical logic here, a logic that goes beyond, while including, the principle of identity and noncontradiction:

> If, for example, purchase and sale — or the metamorphosis of commodities — represent the unity of two processes, or rather the movement of one process through two opposite phases, and thus essentially the unity of the two phases, the movement is essentially just as much the separation of these two phases, and their becoming independent of each other. Since, however, they belong together, the independence of the two correlated aspects can only *show itself* forcibly, as a destructive process. It is just the *crisis* in which they assert their unity, the unity of the different aspects. The independence which these two linked and complimentary phases assume in relation to each other is forcibly destroyed. Thus the crisis manifests the

> unity of the two phases that have become independent of each other. There would be no crisis without this inner unity of factors that are apparently indifferent to each other.[60]

In addition to the use of dialectical logic, Marx shared with Hegel the same theory of universals. "Capital" is a principle of unity, including different forms within it. It is a universal. It even has a certain ontological priority, as is seen in the tendency to crisis that results when one of these forms sets itself up as independent from it. But, Marx repeatedly stressed, Capital is not a "thing." It has no distinct reality apart from the individual forms that it principles. These different forms — the activities of purchase and sale in the marketplace, the process of laboring at the point of production, and so forth — are the "real subjects" of the process.

In the capitalist mode of production, however, the mediation between universal and individual takes on a one-sided form. The reification of universals may lack any ontological foundation. Nonetheless the appearances of such a reification is built into the capitalist system. Inevitably "Capital" seems to take on the characteristics of a thing, itself being the "real subject" of socioeconomic processes. The activities of men and women of flesh and blood — who are in truth the only real subjects — become reduced to mere appearances of an underlying essence, "Capital" in its ceaseless thirst for further accumulation. The life chances of individuals, the economic health of entire communities, the development of nations, now seem to ebb and flow as a function of the needs of "Capital."

As opposed to this alienation, Marx proposed an alternative system. He believed that certain features of the Paris Commune could serve as an anticipation of future socialist societies. Specifically, Marx mentioned with approval the Commune's policy that anyone holding an office in which public power was exercised (whether "political" or "economic") was to be directly elected, subject to recall, and only paid average workers' wages.[61] In this manner decisions regarding production, distribution, and administration would be made by officials directly accountable to the members of society. Extensive public debate would both precede and follow these decisions.

Certain of the philosophical tools Marx derived from Hegel for the analysis of capitalism are applicable here as well. Each individual member of society, of course, is both distinct from and yet united with other individual members. And so a dialectical logic of unity-in-difference would be applicable. Also, the decisions made regarding production, distribution, and administration would establish unity in the society. The content of these decisions thus forms a universal, a unifying principle integrating different individuals under it. And this universal would require a "negation" of finite individuals in two respects. First, no one could expect to get his or her way all of the time. Second, the collective consensus articulated in the decisions would tend to reject the proposals of individuals that were not compatible with universalizable interests.

The universal uniting individuals in socialist democracy is not alien to those individuals in the way that "Capital" is. It is a consensus arrived at by the individuals themselves in the course of ongoing public discussion. It is not imposed upon them by outside forces such as the imperatives of capital accumulation. By participating in the decisions that affect their lives, individuals learn how to transcend their initially private horizon. In the course of public discourse they gradually rise to a wider horizon within which the interests of their fellow citizens are included. Any uncoerced consensus attained "negates" the initial individual interest, to be sure. But it allows a deeper individuality to flourish, an individuality no longer isolated or alienated from the political community. For Marx, only this counts as true autonomy for the individual: "Only within the community has each individual the means of cultivating his gifts in all directions; hence personal freedom becomes possible only within the community."[62]

In capitalism, then, Marx saw an essence ("Capital") that subjects the individuals within it to its imperatives. In council democracy he saw a universal that is reconciled with the autonomy of individuals. *From the perspective of philosophical principles, therefore, Marx's move from capitalism to socialist democracy is exactly parallel to Hegel's move from essence to the notion.* Colletti was correct to stress that in Marxism the finite individual is not swallowed up in any whole *a la* Spinoza. But he has totally failed to grasp that Marx here employed philosophical categories directly derived from that last division of Hegel's *Logic*.

I have argued that Hegel's methodology does not commit him to an eradication of the material incompatible with Marx's thought. For both Hegel and Marx the concrete historical given both was the starting point for thought and retained its autonomy from the thought process, while the thought process was both independent from the real process and had a certain priority over it. I also argued that Hegel's philosophical framework did not commit him to an eradication of the finite individual incompatible with Marxism. Neither Hegel's use of dialectical logic, nor the nature of universals in his system, nor the manner in which he mediated the universal and the individual, leads to this result. And all these features are to be found both in Marx's analysis of capitalism and his proposal for a future society. The central theses of Colletti's book therefore are mistaken. Nonetheless, Hegelianism *is* incompatible with Marxism. And the reasons for this *do* have to do with Hegel's idealism and his views on the autonomy of the finite individual. The reasons just do not lie where Colletti located them.

There are three areas in which Hegel's "idealism" contrasts with Marx's "materialism." Because these areas are well-known, they can be presented briefly here. The first concerns the verification of theories. For Hegel, a thought system can account for its own validity within itself. This explains the circular structure of his system, in which the last category supposedly validates the choice of the first, just as when given the first the last ultimately follows. Marx rejected this idealistic theory of verification; that is, a verification that never leaves the sphere of ideas. His alternative is a verification through material praxis: "The question whether objective truth can be attributed to human thinking is not a question of theory but is a *practical* question. Man must prove the truth, that is, the reality and power, the this-worldliness of his thinking in practice."[63]

A second contrast involves the content of their theories regarding human history. Hegel granted an explanatory primacy in history to systems of ideas. Specifically, the introduction of religious world-views first indicates a new stage in world history. Religious principles subsequently are incorporated in legal, social, economic, and political institutions. For example, Christianity introduced the principle of the modern world:

> This consciousness [that persons are free] arose first in religion, the inmost region of Spirit; but to introduce the principle into the various relations of the actual world, involves a more extensive problem than its simple implantation: a problem whose solution and application require a severe and lengthened process of culture. In proof of this we may note that slavery did not cease immediately on the reception of Christianity. Still less did liberty predominate in States; or Governments and Constitutions adopt a rational organization, or recognize freedom as their basis. That application of the principle to political relations; the thorough moulding and interpenetration of the constitution of society by it, is a process identical with history itself.[64]

> States and Laws are nothing else than Religion manifesting itself in the relations of the actual world.[65]

In Marx's theory of history, systems of ideas such as religious world-views do not have this primacy in historical explanation. Cultural phenomena have no more than a relative autonomy from material socio-economic processes:

> This conception of history thus relies on expounding the real process of production — starting from the material production of life itself — and to comprehending the form of intercourse connected with and created by this mode of production, i.e., civil society in its various stages, as the basis of all history; describing it in its action as the state, and also explaining how all the different theoretical products and forms of consciousness, religion, philosophy, morality, etc., etc., arise from it, and tracing the process of their formation from that basis; thus the whole thing can, of course, be depicted in its totality (and therefore, too, the reciprocal action of these various sides on one another).[66]

The third area in which Hegel's idealism is opposed to Marx's materialism brings us to the other central topic, the question of the autonomy of finite individuals. The common principles employed by Hegel and Marx commit them both to advocating a social system within which universal and individual are united in their difference; that is, the priority of the community does not lead to a sacrifice of the autonomy of individuals. Hegel alone, however, felt that the autonomy of individuals in principle can be preserved within the modern capitalist system. In his model of that system Hegel included certain features to guarantee this: individual rights to property, the individual child's right to education, the individual's right to free speech and to various other civil rights such as a fair and public trial by peers according to public laws, and so on.[67] Hegel therefore was intellectually reconciled with the modern capitalist state. His attitude toward it was the contemplative ("idealistic") one of appreciating its inner rationality.

For Marx, the measures listed by Hegel are totally incapable of guaranteeing the autonomy of individuals within the political community. As long as the society is subject to the imperatives of capital accumulation, measures like property rights instead allow the exploitation of one class over another. This exploitation both negates the individual autonomy of the members of the exploited classes and prevents a true universal, one incorporating the interests of all, from being articulated. Marx's theory therefore culminates with a call to a praxis that transforms the material conditions to create a material reality in which the universal (the community) is truly united with the autonomy of the individuals within it. This call to material praxis is the third and perhaps the most important area in which Marx defended a materialism not to be found in Hegel.

VI

Elster's Critique of Marx's Systematic Dialectical Theory

For decades theorists within the analytical tradition of social theory have expressed hostility to dialectical methodology.[1] A number of analytical Marxists[2] today share this judgment. In the first section of this chapter I contrast John Roemer's blanket condemnation of dialectical social theory with Jon Elster's position. Elster was willing to concede that there is one type of dialectical theory that can be translated into acceptable terms. However, Elster vehemently rejected the type of dialectical theory that has been the main focus of this book, that concerned with systematic derivations. In the second section I present Elster's main arguments against this sort of dialectical theory. In the third section I respond to these objections. My thesis is that Elster has failed to provide compelling reasons to reject the dialectical theory of socioeconomic categories presented by Marx in works such as the *Grundrisse* and *Capital*.

Roemer's Critique of Dialectical Laws in History

Dialectical methodology in social theory usually is associated with teleological explanations of history. Hegel saw history as an ordered sequence of stages, each of which represents a moment in the unfolding of spirit. In the earliest historical stages spirit is undeveloped and merely potential. At the culmination of history the socioeconomic realm, the state, and the cultural sphere have all attained a form commensurate with the full development of spirit. If we ask why any specific historical stage occurred, Hegel would point to the necessary role that stage played in the process of spirit's development from potentiality to actuality. Dialectical method traces the impact of dialectical laws and the overcoming of dialectical contradictions in this historical progression. In this manner each stage is assigned its proper role in this development.

Marx, of course, rejected the idealism of Hegel's philosophy of history. For Marx history ultimately is not a process of the unfolding of spirit, but rather a sequence of modes of production. Whatever the differences in content separating Hegel and Marx, however, the form of their historical theories is quite similar. For Marx each mode of production plays a necessary role in the development of the human species. In early stages of history the low level of productive power and the rigidity of social organizations prevented human capacities from flourishing. In the future stage of social evolution, socialism, the material and social preconditions of human flourishing will be guaranteed to all. If we ask why a specific stage of history has occurred, Marx would point to the necessary role that stage played in the progression to socialism. The dialectic of history may be a materialist dialectic in Marx's hands. But it remains a methodology by means of which each stage is assigned its necessary role in a teleological process of development. And Marx too felt that there were dialectical laws underlying this development, laws that were manifest in the contradictions and overcoming of contradictions that make up history.

John Roemer is one of the leading figures in analytical Marxism. He vehemently rejected the notion of a dialectical logic immanent in history:

> Too often, obscurantism protects itself behind a yoga of special terms and privileged logic. The yoga of Marxism is 'dialectics.' Dialectical logic is based on several propositions which may have a certain inductive appeal, but are far from being rules of inference: that things turn into their opposites, and quantity turns into quality. In Marxian social science, dialectics is often used to justify a lazy kind of teleological reasoning.[3]

Rational choice Marxists have a clear alternative to dialectical methodology: the tools of mainstream social science. They hold that whatever Marx had to say that remains of interest can be formulated in the terms of game theory and neoclassical economics. Anything that cannot be formulated in these terms is not acceptable social science and must be rejected. More specifically the global claims of Marxism must be provided with adequate microfoundations at the level of the rational choices of individuals. Global teleologies typically do without such microfoundations and therefore must be abandoned.

At this point there does not seem to be much room for dialogue between rational choice Marxism and dialectical Marxism. However, Jon Elster, the other leading representative of rational choice Marxism, has pushed the exchange forward. In his discussion of dialectics he made two points that go beyond Roemer. First, Elster held that reference to so-called dialectical laws and dialectical contradictions does have a proper role in social science, albeit a restricted one. Regarding the transformation of quantity into quality, for instance, Elster points out that this "law" provides a reminder that the functional link between an independent variable and a dependent variable may be discontinuous and nonlinear.[4]

Elster also discovered a rational kernel in the concept of real contradictions. Social agents all too often commit the fallacy of composition; that is, they jump from believing that a description that may be true of *any* agent could be true of *all*. When this occurs their actions usually will not attain the results intended, a situation Elster termed *counterfinality*. Elster believed that Hegel and Marx were groping toward the notion of counterfinality when they insisted that there are real contradictions in history.[5]

This partial rehabilitation of dialectics within social science is of considerable interest. However I shall not pursue this topic here. Instead I concentrate on another point made by Elster in this context. Elster pointed out that dialectical theory is a genus with two different species. We have been considering one of these species, the explication of dialectical laws and contradictions in history. The other species is termed by Elster *dialectical deduction*.

This distinction is familiar to us from Chapter III. Hegel attempted to uncover a dialectic in history in his unpublished lectures on the philosophy of history, the history of religion, the history of art, and so on. However, in his published works, such as *The Science of Logic* and *The Philosophy of Right*, Hegel traced the systematic derivation of a series of categories, rather than a sequence of historical stages. And he insisted that the logical order and the historical order could not be equated.

Turning to Marx, there are numerous works in which he does appear to claim that the essence of history is captured in an unfolding dialectic. But as I have argued throughout this work, in many other places his aim is the dialectical deduction of thought determinations; that is, a logical rather than a historical progression.

Although Elster did not bring out the point, it is important to note that Roemer's objections to dialectics do not touch this second species of dialectical theory. Theories based on dialectical deductions are still teleological in a certain sense. They progress forward until the goal of the theory has been attained with the derivation of the last category. But this sort of teleology in no way commits one to teleological explanations of specific occurrences in empirical history. And this was the basis for Roemer's rejection of dialectical Marxism.

If this were the end of the matter we might conclude that dialectical Marxism and rational choice Marxism could peacefully coexist in a theoretical division of labor. Those operating within the latter paradigm could concern themselves with providing the microfoundations for claims in empirical social science, acknowledging that dialectical considerations have a restricted role to play here, at least when "restated in ordinary 'analytical' language."[6] Representatives of the former perspective could accept this restricted role in social science, turning the remainder of their efforts to a quite different sort of theory, systematic dialectical deduction. However this reconciliation of the two positions is rather premature, to put it mildly. For in Elster's view the second sort of dialectical theory is completely illegitimate; in fact, it is "barely intelligible."[7]

Elster's Critique of Deductive Dialectical Theory

Elster held that when considering dialectical derivations "one encounters the familiar difficulty of refuting a confused position which, by its very incoherence, resists being pinned down sufficiently to allow a precise rebuttal." His strategy is "to mount attacks from several quarters, in the hope that their cumulative impact will prove persuasive."[8] Elster mounts seven such attacks.

1. Hegel's *Science of Logic* can be taken as the paradigm case of a deductive dialectical theory. In Elster's view Hegel "derived the various ontological categories from each other according to certain deductive principles which have resisted analysis to this day. The connection is neither that of cause to effect, nor that of axiom to theorem, nor finally that of given fact to its condition of possibility."[9] He implied that the same condemnation can be made of all such theories, including the portions of Marx's work that fit under this heading.

2. If deductive dialectical theories do not follow any explicit principles of deduction, then it follows that they are *ad hoc*. Again referring to the *Science of Logic* Elster wrote that, "The 'self-determination of the concept' appears to be nothing more than a loose *ex post* pattern imposed by Hegel on various phenomena that he found important."[10] Elster would dismiss Marx's attempts to trace the "self-development of capital" on the same grounds.

3. The next criticism connects dialectical deductions with the holism so vehemently rejected by rational choice Marxists: "The defects of the conceptual deduction are linked to those of methodological collectivism. It is, in fact, difficult to decide whether the self-determination of capital is conceptual or behavioural — or whether we are meant to conclude that this very distinction is superseded."[11]

4. Hegel's deduction of ontological categories in the *Logic* and elsewhere clearly is distinct from a presentation of different stages in history. When we turn to works by Marx such as the *Grundrisse* and *Capital*, however, things are more complicated and more incoherent: "Unlike the Hegelian categories, the economic ones also succeed each other chronologically, in the order of their historical appearance. Hence Marx had to confront the question of how the logical sequence is related to the historical one, without being able, however, to provide a consistent answer"[12]

5. Elster next turned to the specific categories proposed by Marx at the beginning of both the *Grundrisse* and *Capital*. We find there the following sequence: product - commodity - exchange value - money - capital - labor. Elster argued that this sequence "makes some empirical sense" when it is taken as a historical interpretation, although it does not provide an "explanation of what drives the process, only a fancy redescription of the successive stages." However if this sequence is read as a logicodialectical deduction, as Marx seems to have intended at least some of the time, then it "remains vacuous."[13]

6. Elster next considers the transition from money to capital more closely. Elster quotes a passage from the *Grundrisse*[14] in which money is interpreted in terms of Hegel's logical category of "quantity." Pure quantity has no intrinsic limit; it always is possible to find a number greater than any given number. Marx interpreted money as an instance of this logical structure of pure quantity. Therefore money can have no intrinsic limit; money always tends to increase beyond any given quantitative barrier. Because money that increases after it has been invested is by definition capital, Marx concluded that the transition from money to

capital is immanent within the concept of money. Elster accused Marx of both obscurity and a conceptual slight of hand here. He insisted that the transition from money to capital can be explained only in terms of the emergence of the reinvestment motive in early capitalism. And as Max Weber well knew, this could be done only with reference to the motives of individual economic agents. "It cannot be derived from a conceptual analysis of money."[15]

7. The next stage in Marx's progression of categories, and the final one considered by Elster in this context, is the transition from capital to the exploitation of wage labor. Elster presented Marx's argument as follows. *Capital* refers by definition to an economy in which the money accumulated at the end of production and exchange exceeds the initial money invested; that is, there is an economywide surplus. The exploitation of labor power is the condition of the possibility for this general surplus in the economy. Therefore a transition from "capital" to "the exploitation of wage labor" must be made. Elster commented that "The deduction is invalid, since any commodity may be taken as the one whose exploitation makes the economy productive and hence makes a surplus possible."[16]

In the next section I address each of these points in turn.

Replies to Elster's Criticisms

Objection 1

For Hegel, philosophical thinking occurs whenever thought takes itself as its object. This means that the fundamental categories employed in everyday life, in the scientific study of nature and society, and in religious and metaphysical beliefs are considered explicitly in themselves. The philosopher then attempts to connect these categories systematically: "Speaking generally, to deal with anything in a speculative or philosophical way simply means to bring into connection the thoughts which we already have."[17] Elster was quite correct that the connection among categories in this type of dialectical theory is neither cause-effect, axiom-theorem, nor fact-condition of possibility. But he was mistaken to conclude that there is no determinate principle for the ordering of the categories. As I noted numerous times in previous chapters, the connection stems from the fact that not all categories fall on the same level of generality. Some categories define ontological (or natural, or social, or religious, etc.) structures that are simple and abstract. Others define structures that include the content of more simple and abstract categories, while adding some further determination to them. These categories thus are more complex and concrete than the first. Hegel's project is a step-by-step progression of categories moving from the simplest and most abstract categories to those that are the most complex and concrete. In this context dialectical logic is nothing more than the set of rules that operate when transitions from simple and abstract categories to complex and concrete ones are made.[18]

In his systematic writings Marx followed a similar procedure. In these works his aim was to reconstruct in thought the capitalist mode of production. He began with this mode of production as it was given in both everyday experience and the theories of political economy. He separated out the most abstract categories operative here. Then he proceeded to move step-by-step to ever more concrete determinations. Let us recall once again the Introduction to the *Grundrisse*, Marx's most explicit discussion of methodological matters, where he clearly stated that this was his procedure:

> I [would] begin with...a chaotic conception of the whole, and I would then, by means of further determination, move...towards ever more simple concepts, from the imagined concrete towards ever thinner abstractions until I had arrived at the simplest determinations. From there the journey would have to be retraced until I had finally arrived at the [concrete] again, but this time not as the chaotic conception of a whole, but as a rich totality of many determinations and relations.[19]

Interestingly, Elster later did acknowledge that Marx's theory moves on different levels of abstraction according to what Elster terms "the method of successive approximations."[20] However he never considered the possibility that this might provide a principle for deriving categorial connections. He did not recognize that his list of the possible principles for categorial connections (cause-effect, axiom-theorem, and fact-condition of possibility) cannot be taken as exhaustive.[21]

Objection 2

To some extent Elster's second objection already has been answered. A theory that systematically moves from simple and abstract categories to determinations that are progressively more complex and concrete cannot proceed in an *ad hoc* fashion. If a simpler category were to follow a more complex one, this clearly would be methodologically illegitimate. However we can go further in specifying how the derivations within systematic dialectical theories are to be made. Because the topic of this book concerns dialectical social theory, I shall limit the discussion to derivations within this type of dialectical theory.

In a dialectical social theory we begin with an abstract thought determination. This category defines an abstract social form. Examination of the social form defined by this category may reveal that certain structural tendencies are necessarily built into that social form. This does not mean that a specific event or process must necessarily occur whenever the social form in question is given. But it does mean that if this social form is given it is necessarily the case that the probability of specific sorts of events or processes occurring is considerably higher than the probability of their not occurring. The phrase *considerably higher* admittedly is rather vague, but it is sufficient for our purposes.

Next, it may be the case that were these structural tendencies to occur they would necessarily tend to generate a social form distinct from that with which we initially began. If this is the case, then there is a systematic necessity to introduce a new category into the theory, one that defines this new social form. This later category "sublates" the earlier one; that is, it includes its content while adding some new determination that goes beyond what was present in the earlier category. In this manner a necessary transition from one category to another is derived. The sequence of such transitions makes up a systematic progression of determinations reconstructing the given social realm in thought.

I do not claim that neither Hegel nor Marx ever made *ad hoc* derivations. But if the legitimacy of a methodology rested on the impossibility of introducing extraneous considerations, *no* methodology would count as legitimate. What does matter is that if extraneous considerations are introduced our methodological precepts allow us to recognize that this has occurred and to correct matters. *Pace* Elster, the methodology described in the previous paragraph provides such guidance.[22]

Objection 3

What is the connection between systematic dialectical theories and methodological collectivism? It is true that dialectical social theories do present a progression of social forms, and these are macro-level structures. And it is also the case that these social forms are viewed as conditioning the behavior of social agents. However the methodology of dialectical social theories does not in principle involve a commitment to the thesis that these social forms themselves "act" in any sense (although it is true that Hegel all too often used misleading action language when discussing the forms defined by the categories of his theory). More specifically, dialectical methodology does not imply a claim that one social form "generates" another in the progression of social forms. The accusation of methodological collectivism thus does not seem to be warranted.

How are categorial transitions made? A transition from one social form to another can be introduced if and only if it can be shown that agents operating under the first social form necessarily would tend to act in a manner that brought about the second. In other words, categorial transitions are warranted if and only if microfoundations regarding the behavior of social agents could be provided. Of course Hegel and Marx had no access to the techniques of game theory or mathematical economics. Nonetheless the concern for microfoundations characteristic of rational choice Marxism has a significant role to play in dialectical social theory.[23]

This allows us to answer Elster's question regarding whether social theories based on dialectical deductions are conceptual or behavioral. They are both at once. There is a conceptual progression from one category defining a relatively abstract social form to another fixing a more concrete one. And this progression is bound up with the answer to the following question: how would social agents tend to behave were they to operate within the given social form?

It is not generally appreciated how dialectical social theorists such as Marx and Hegel sought microfoundations when motivating categorial transitions. Some examples from *Capital* will be discussed later. Here a typical transition from Hegel's *Philosophy of Right*, already sketched in Chapter IV, may be cited as an example. The category "contract" defines a social form within which persons, having objectified their will in external objects, mutually agree to an exchange of those objects. The next category in Hegel's systematic progression is "wrong." In motivating this transition Hegel explicitly provided the required microfoundations. On the quite abstract categorial level of contract the exchanging parties are motivated by self-interest alone, and no legal framework for resolving disputes is present. Given these parameters, Hegel asserted, social agents necessarily would tend to act such that cases of non-malicious wrong, fraud, and crime would arise. The categorial transition is justified in terms of the behavior of social agents under the given parameters.[24]

Just as it often is overlooked that dialectical theorists must provide microfoundations for their categorial transitions, it also is overlooked that rational choice Marxists cannot avoid references to social forms. Before the question of individual and group decisions can even be formulated, rational choice theorists first must situate social agents within a context. This is done through defining the axioms and setting the parameters of a model. Some of these axioms and parameters will refer to the behavioral dispositions of individuals. But if the theory is to have any determinate content, axioms and parameters specifying social forms inevitably will be introduced as well, social forms that condition the action of individuals and groups. In the writings of Elster and Roemer, for instance, what Marx termed the *commodity form*, the *money form*, and so on are introduced into their models in this fashion. As soon as this is done we no longer have a social ontology limited to social agents. Social forms that are in some sense distinct from those agents also claim ontological status (although, of course, these forms are brought about and reproduced through the actions of social agents).

Nor can rational choice theorists deny that social forms condition individuals and groups to tend to act in certain ways rather than others. If that were ruled out, rational choice theorists themselves would not be able to derive any determinate results from the axioms and parameters of their models. Elster's third objection therefore is no more justified than the first two.

The three objections just considered were directed against the project of systematic dialectical theories in general. The remaining objections are of a different nature. The four to be considered next are specifically directed against Marx's attempt to construct this sort of theory in the *Grundrisse* and *Capital*. It should be kept in mind, therefore, that even if all four criticisms were valid, this would not imply that systematic dialectical theories in principle are illegitimate.

Objection 4

Elster's fourth criticism was that the relationship between historical developments and logical derivations was never clarified in the *Grundrisse* and *Capital*. Sometimes when Marx appeared to be deriving a logical sequence of social forms he would abruptly shift to language suggesting a description of a sequence of stages in history. And sometimes he would do the reverse.

Because this issue was the topic of Chapter III, I can be fairly brief in replying to Elster. Marx did periodically juxtapose statements referring to a sequence of historical stages with statements regarding the systematic connection among categories. But this can be seen as primarily a rhetorical strategy. Marx's historical digressions in his systematic writings were designed to address readers with no special interest in systematic dialectical theory. The fact that Marx was willing to make these digressions does not at all prove that he did not consistently distinguish the logical order from the systematic order. The following passage shows that this distinction was quite clear to him:

> It would be unfeasible and wrong to let the economic categories follow one another in the same sequence as that in which they were historically decisive. Their sequence is determined rather by their relation to one another in modern bourgeois society.... The point is not the historic position of the economic relations in the succession of different forms of society...[25]

Even if Marx were clear about the general distinction, it could still be the case that in specific sections of his theory the systematic and the historical were confused. This brings us to the fifth objection.

Objection 5

Elster made two points regarding the initial progression of categories in Marx's systematic theory. First, he granted that the ordering Marx proposed has a certain historical plausibility, even if it is a mere redescription of the historical process and not an explanation of it. Second, he insisted that as a logicodeductive dialectic the ordering is "vacuous." Neither comment is on the mark.[26]

In interpreting the progression "product — commodity — exchange value — money — capital" as "a historical sequence, generated by ordinary causal processes rather than by dialectics"[27] Elster maps each category to a stage in the following historical development:

1. Production oriented to the subsistence needs of the producers within a community;

2. The emergence of trade among different communities;

3. The regularization of this external trade, such that part of production is devoted to the production of commodities with exchange value;

4. The generalization of commodity production, with merchant capital directing its attention to intracommunity exchange;

5. The emergence of production for surplus value.

However plausible this latter sequence of stages might be as historical narrative, the attempt to reduce Marx's categorial progression to this narrative fails for a number of reasons.

The starting point of *Capital* and the *Grundrisse* is not a community producing to meet its own needs; neither is it a community engaged in either sporadic or regular trade with its neighbors. In these works Marx followed the procedure sketched in the Introduction to the *Grundrisse*. He began with the totality that is the capitalist mode of production, abstracted out its simplest determinations, and then progressed in a step-by-step fashion to more complex and concrete determinations of that mode of production. Marx could hardly have been more explicit about his starting point. The very first paragraph of *Capital* states, "The wealth of those societies in which the capitalist mode of production prevails, presents itself as 'an immense accumulation of commodities,' its unit being a single commodity. Our investigation must therefore begin with the analysis of a commodity."[28] In other words, Marx's goal was to provide a systematic reconstruction in thought of a historical phenomenon, not a historical account of the genesis of that phenomenon.

Second, in Elster's reading the category "value" appears to be connected with the historical epoch of simple commodity production, a transitional period between capitalism and feudalism. However, Marx is quite insistent that the category of value is "entirely peculiar" to modern capitalism: "The concept of value is entirely peculiar to the most modern economy, since it is the most abstract expression of capital itself and of the production resting on it."[29] This strongly suggests that "value" (and other categories at the beginning of the theory) are to be taken as abstract determinations of developed capitalism and not concrete determinations of some precapitalist historical stage.

The third point also concerns the notion of value. In the beginning of Marx's systematic economic works this category defines a social form in which the exchange of commodities is governed exclusively by the amount of socially necessary abstract labor time required for the production of the commodities. However there has *never* been a historical epoch in which the exchange of goods has been governed by value in this immediate manner. In both precapitalism and early capitalism exchange ratios have been affected by factors such as the time necessary to take goods to market, fluctuations in effective demand, the interventions of the state, and so on. Marx, an intellectual giant in the study of economic history, was well aware of this. We must conclude that the category "value" is won through abstracting from these complicating factors rather than from early stages in economic history.

Fourth, we should recall that if we want to see Marx's story regarding the historical genesis of capitalism there are better places for us to turn than the initial categories of Marx's theory. Marx interrupted the systematic progression of categories in *Capital* to discuss the process of original accumulation. Here we find his account of the transition from feudalism to capitalism spelled out in great detail. If Marx already had presented his account of this transition at the beginning of *Capital*, as Elster supposed, why would he then spend a hundred pages at the end of volume 1 to cover the same ground? It is much more plausible to assume that the beginning of volume 1 has a quite different theoretical purpose.

Finally, in the fourth historical stage discussed by Elster, reference is made to merchant capital. But merchant capital plays no role whatsoever at the beginning of Marx's systematic economic theory. Accordingly, Elster is forced in this context to refer to volume 3 of *Capital*, even though his historical sequence is supposed to correspond to the initial categories of volume 1.[30] Marx quite clearly felt that merchant capital was a much more concrete and complex category than those considered at the beginning of volume 1. This undermines Elster's attempt to find a place for it alongside such simple and abstract categories as "commodity," "value," and "money."

We already noted that Elster was well aware of Marx's method of successive approximations. Why then did he ignore this method and introduce a historical method when interpreting Marx's initial categories? We have seen the answer already: he regarded the historical interpretation as plausible and the systematic reading as vacuous. The former view cannot be substantiated. Are his arguments for the latter any more convincing?

The transition to the money form and the capital form will be discussed later. Here I consider the prior transition from the commodity form to the value form. Elster had two main criticisms of this transition. First, Marx cannot claim that the move to the labor theory of value necessarily follows from a consideration of the commodity form. It is possible to have commodities produced and sold within a totally automated economy. In this case the very notion of labor value is senseless. It is also the case that even when commodities are produced by means of labor they may share some other feature in common, and this other feature might better explain their exchangeability as commodities. Elster mentioned utility as a common feature that undercuts the necessity of introducing labor values.[31]

The second objection is that the category of value is not an adequate principle for the derivation of later categories in the theory such as "equilibrium prices." Given the wage rate and the technological coefficients prices can be derived without any reference to value, and the attempt to derive equilibrium prices from value inevitably breaks down.[32]

Elster's first criticism overlooks a central feature of Marx's systematic theory. Marx's objective was to reconstruct in thought a specific mode of production, the capitalist mode of production. Therefore the initial determinations in his theory must be specific to that mode of production. Marx explicitly considered a totally automated economy.[33] However he insisted that it must be seen as a radical break with capitalism and not as a mere variant of it. The defining social relation of capitalism, the capital-wage labor relation, is not present. Also, it hardly can be said that Marx was unaware that utility was a common feature of commodities.[34] However utility is a common feature of goods and services circulated within *all* economic systems. Hence this category can play only a subordinate role if our goal is to understand a mode of production in its historical specificity.

The second objection here is quite a bit more controversial than Elster suggests. Anwar Shaikh has presented a strong case suggesting that the quantitative connection between values and profits is much closer than Elster and others were willing to concede.[35] However for our purposes this question can be left open. The categorial ordering presented by Marx does not rest on the results of mathematical economics, however important these results may be in other contexts.

Starting from the concept of "commodity," Marx justified the transition to the category "value" in the following manner. Social agents operating under the commodity form engage in the production of commodities privately; that is, there is no *ex ante* coordination of production. They subsequently must prove that their privately undertaken labor was socially necessary. The proof comes when the products of that labor are successfully sold. Under these conditions it is necessarily the case that there will tend to be a difference between privately undertaken labor that is socially necessary and that which is not. It therefore is necessarily the case that we must introduce a new category to capture this distinction. That category is "value"; only privately undertaken labor that proves its social necessity creates value. In this sense the value form sublates the commodity form; it includes the latter while adding a further determination to it.

The transition to the money form follows at once. Social agents operating within the above context would necessarily tend to introduce money both as an external measure of the socially necessary labor claimed to be manifested in the commodity and as a means of circulation that allows the exchange of commodities to function more smoothly. Finally, "price" is nothing but the money form of commodities after complicating factors abstracted from on the initial level of the theory have been introduced. In this qualitative sense "price" *is* derived from "value."[36]

We must conclude that Elster has failed in his attempt to establish that the logicodialectical derivation of the initial determinations of Marx's theory is vacuous. When this is combined with his failure to provide a plausible historical reading of the beginning of *Capital*, his fifth reason to reject systematic dialectics can be set aside.

Objection 6

Elster's objection to the next transition in Marx's dialectical social theory, the move from money to capital, is marred in two fundamental respects. First, he believed that Marx had to account for the motivations of the agents responsible for the historical genesis of this mode of production. But as we already noted on numerous occasions, Marx's main project in the *Grundrisse* and *Capital* was to reconstruct the capitalist mode of production in thought. He *began* with the fact that this mode of production had arisen and then attempted to understand it through an ordering of its fundamental categories. The transition from "money" to "capital" is a stage in this systematic reconstruction rather than part of a story regarding the historical genesis of capitalism.

The second difficulty in Elster's account is that he failed to comprehend the systematic motivation for the transition that Marx provided. It is true that Marx invoked Hegel's category of pure quantity, and it is also true that this fails to account for the transition. (At most it accounts for an ontological possibility: insofar as money is measured quantitatively it always is possible in principle for an increment to be added to any given sum of money.) The reference to Hegel's category of quantity indeed does fail to provide the microfoundations for the transition. Marx, however, did provide such microfoundations.

Let us begin with the money form. The category "money" is first introduced as a measure of value and then as a medium of exchange in a process where social agents sell commodities they do not need to obtain money to be used to purchase commodities they do require. This $C \rightarrow M \rightarrow C$ circuit can be interrupted due to the vagaries of the market. For instance, social agents may not find buyers for extended periods of time. When this occurs they will not be able to obtain the money required to purchase needed commodities. Rational agents will anticipate this and attempt to acquire money funds to hold them over in such periods. In this manner Marx introduced the notion of money as end of exchange, the $M \rightarrow C \rightarrow M$ circuit. However, rational social agents operating under this social form generally would not be content to acquire a money fund equivalent to that with which they began. Hence it is necessarily the case that there is a structural tendency to move to a $M \rightarrow C \rightarrow M^1$ circuit, where the agents aim at acquiring an incremental increase of money at the conclusion of exchange. The $M \rightarrow C \rightarrow M^1$ circulation process includes the $M \rightarrow C \rightarrow M$ circuit, while adding a new determination that goes beyond it. The category "capital," defined in terms of the $M \rightarrow C \rightarrow M^1$ circuit, thus must follow the category "money" in the dialectical progression of socioeconomic categories.[37]

Here again the problem is not that Elster was unaware of Marx's position. He noted that Marx held the views on money mentioned in the preceding paragraph. Once again the problem is instead Elster's lack of sympathy for systematic theory. He discussed this part of Marx's theory solely in the context of the historical instability of simple commodity production.[38] He failed to even consider the possibility that this might be of relevance to the dialectical derivation of the capital form from the money form.

Objection 7

The last objection formulated by Elster was that Marx's next transition, the move from capital to the exploitation of wage labor, cannot be accepted. Elster rested his case on the point that the same sort of argument used in mathematical economics to establish the exploitation of wage labor also can be used to establish the exploitation of other inputs into production as well. The arguments for a "steel theory of exploitation" are no less valid than those for a theory of the exploitation of wage labor.

Three points are to be made in reply. First, this argument overlooks the essential task of Marx's theory. *Capital* presents a dialectic of *social* forms, a theory of *social* relations. Even if from a formal mathematical standpoint the exploitation of corn and the exploitation of wage labor are identical, when the theoretical objective is to understand the dynamic of the social relations that make up capitalism, the latter alone is of interest.

Second, Elster had a quite narrow interpretation of the concept of exploitation. In his usage it referred simply to the extraction of an economic surplus from a production input. But for Marx two conditions must hold before an institutional arrangement could be termed exploitative: a surplus must be extracted *and* the producers of this surplus must lack the ability to control the allocation of this surplus. Consider the two stages of communism sketched by Marx in *The Critique of the Gotha Program*.[39] Elster would have to say that workers are exploited in both stages. They produce a surplus that is then allocated to the maintenance and expansion of the means of production and to the provision of public consumption goods. For Marx it would be nonsense to see exploitation here. The crucial thing is not that a surplus is extracted from workers, but that the producers themselves control the allocation of this surplus through workers' councils.

If we employ this broader and more accurate definition of exploitation, then the "steel theory of exploitation" can be dismissed at once. Although economic surplus can be extracted from inputs such as steel, it would be a crass category mistake to attempt to ask whether steel had control of the appropriated surplus. In the sense of the term relevant here *control* is applicable only to a specific exercise of human subjectivity. Complaining that steel lacked control over an extracted surplus would be as meaningless as complaining that the poor bicycle does not get to choose the direction of its travel.[40]

Finally, it is interesting to note that whereas both Elster and Roemer criticized Marx for overlooking the possibility of other inputs being exploited, when it came time for them to propose their own theories of exploitation this point was forgotten. In the entire chapter devoted to exploitation in Elster's *Making Sense of Marx*, the exploitation of social agents is the only topic discussed. The same holds for Roemer's *A General Theory of Exploitation and Class*. They are completely correct to concentrate exclusively on exploitation as a social matter, but they can then hardly fault Marx for doing likewise.

Concluding Remarks

I argued that the objections made by analytical Marxists against both systematic dialectical theories in general and the beginning of Marx's systematic theory in specific are not convincing. Of course it is always open to the critics of dialectical Marxism to reformulate these objections or propose new ones. But another response is possible as well, the response of indifference. Analytical Marxists could assert that the question of the internal cogency of systematic dialectical methodology is entirely secondary. However this question is answered, they might say, dialectical social theory should be abandoned. All our attention should be directed instead toward revising the Marxist perspective in the light of the techniques of game theory and neoclassical economics. In conclusion I would like to suggest two reasons why analytical Marxists should not be so quick to deny the importance of systematic dialectical theory.

Reason 1

To the extent that analytical Marxists wish to examine Marx on his own terms, they must take systematic dialectics seriously. Otherwise they will propose views on Marx that are thoroughly misguided. There are a number of places where analytical Marxists have formulated objections to Marx based on a lack of comprehension of the nature of his theory. I have already pointed to some places where Elster's hostility to systematic dialectical theory led him to misinterpret Marx. The next chapter will be devoted to another example, Roemer's criticism of Marx's theory of exploitation in capitalism.

Reason 2

Let us grant that an appreciation of systematic dialectical theory is necessary for a proper interpretation of Marx's writings. Is there any other reason to consider this type of theory significant? Are there tasks that systematic social theories can accomplish better than other sorts of theories? I conclude by mentioning four points that suggest this unfashionable theory type may yet have a role to play today.

First, in empirical social science, categories often are employed without being clarified. The conceptual clarification that does occur often is *ad hoc*, as the social scientists select out some categories for mention and ignore others. The project of constructing a systematic progression of categories helps us employ categories in our empirical work in a reflective fashion, and it forces us to do so in a comprehensive manner.

In this context it is interesting to note that a social scientist as hostile to dialectical Marxism as Max Weber implicitly recognized this. The beginning of his *magnum opus*, *Economy and Society*, can be read as his attempt to reconstruct the fundamental categories of social theory in a systematic fashion, moving from the most simple and abstract determination ("Social Action") to more complex and concrete categories (e.g., "Political and Hierocratic Organizations").[41]

All social theorists should be sympathetic to the goal of conceptual clarification. There are three further goals of systematic dialectical theory that Marxists should be especially sympathetic towards. These goals already have been mentioned in Chapter III, and so I only discuss them briefly here.

Second, economic categories that reflect the way capitalism appears in everyday experience have a very strong hold on the mind. And yet these appearances can hide essential features of this system. A systematic reconstruction in which categories reflecting concrete appearances are derived from categories that fix the fundamental social forms of capitalism can help dispel illusions generated by the manner in which capitalism appears in everyday experience.

Third, it is possible to distinguish structural tendencies that necessarily follow once specific social forms are given from the concrete events, processes, and structures of empirical history. The latter are permeated with contingency in a way the former are not. Any specific event, process, or structure always could have been different had circumstances been changed. For example, specific details concerning the relationship between this particular set of capitalists and that group of wage laborers depend on a myriad of more or less accidental factors, regarding which we can formulate empirical claims. But the claim that capitalists tend to exploit wage laborers is rather different. If Marx was correct, that claim does not depend on accidental factors. It follows necessarily from the capital form. Given the distinct nature of these types of claims, it makes some sense to consider claims of necessity of this sort separately from more contingent sorts of claims.

Dialectical social theory cannot replace empirical social science. In fact, it is parasitical on social science, because arguments establishing necessary structural tendencies demand considerable empirical knowledge. Nonetheless, it does provide us with the distinct sort of theory we are seeking. We have seen that the categories of a dialectical social theory define social forms and that the categorial transitions in the theory are motivated in terms of the structural tendencies that necessarily arise when social agents operate within those forms. This implies that a comprehensive progression of categories simultaneously provides a comprehensive set of the structural tendencies that are necessarily given within the object realm. This provides another reason for regarding systematic dialectical theory as significant.

Finally, there is also a practical consideration. Systematic dialectical theories can orient praxis. More specifically, they provide theoretical guidance for revolutionary politics.

Revolutionary politics can be defined in terms of the commitment to transform fundamental social structures. This presupposes that fundamental structures can be distinguished from those that are not fundamental. A dialectical ordering of social forms allows us to make this distinction. For example, when Marx showed how the categories "rent" and "bank capital" can be derived dialectically from the capital form, he provided an argument for seeing the latter as a more fundamental structure than the first two phenomena. This allowed him to ground a distinction between two forms of praxis: the revolutionary overthrow of the capital form, on the one hand, and reformist tinkering with rent control or bank regulations, on the other.

It may be that other sorts of theory also can help us clarify the basic categories we employ, dispel illusions arising from everyday experience, formulate claims of necessity, and orient revolutionary politics. I have not established that it is mandatory for Marxists to concern themselves with this sort of theory, only that this sort of theory is both permissible and significant. The dismissal of systematic dialectics on the part of rational choice Marxists must be abandoned.

VII

Roemer on Marx's Theory of Exploitation: Shortcomings of a Non-Dialectical Approach

In a number of recent books and papers the analytical Marxist John Roemer presented a series of objections to the Marxist category of exploitation. In the first section of this chapter I consider his four central criticisms. The second section consists of a summary of Marx's systematic dialectical methodology and the main categories introduced in the beginning of *Capital*. In the concluding section each of Roemer's objections is replied to in turn. I argue that Roemer's arguments are flawed due to his failure to appreciate the nature of systematic dialectical theory.

Roemer's Criticisms

For Roemer, Marx's notion of exploitation in capitalism is defined in terms of surplus labor extracted from the working class at the point of production by the capitalist class. In the production process the working class creates a quantity of economic value through its labor. However, the wages paid do not reflect the value created by this labor, but only the value of the commodity labor power, a significantly smaller quantity. Workers thus create surplus value through their surplus labor, which then is appropriated by the capitalists who purchased their labor power.

Four main objections of Roemer against this position are considered here. First, Roemer objected that Marx's notion of exploitation is not defensible by itself. Second, he claimed that Marx did not recognize that there can be surplus labor extraction without exploitation. Third, Marx supposedly also failed to grasp that there can be exploitation without surplus labor extraction. Finally, Roemer held that emphasis on exploitation in Marx's theory distracts us from what is of central normative significance in social life. Let us consider these objections in turn.

"Exploitation" Cannot Stand Alone

According to Roemer, Marx's category "exploitation" is fundamentally incomplete. Neoclassical economists assert that surplus labor extraction in capitalism is generally *not* exploitative because workers simply are exchanging their labor for access to capital. If this perspective is to be answered, the definition of "exploitation" must go beyond the mere notion of surplus labor extraction:

> One might say that the ownership of capital by the capitalist is unjust in the first place, and hence the worker should not have to give up anything to have access to it. From the formal point of view, however, invoking aspects of property relations is *ad hoc* if one adheres to the labor theory of value definition of exploitation: if property relations must be invoked, they should either be built into the definition or implied by it.[1]

Surplus Labor Extraction Can Occur Without Exploitation

Roemer constructed the following now-famous thought experiment to illustrate this point.[2] Suppose a three-person economy with corn as the only product. A limited amount of corn capital is available in the economy, say 1 unit, that can be used as an input into a corn production process. When it is employed in factory production, ⅔ unit of seed corn and eight hours labor are required to produce an amount of corn (*b*) necessary to satisfy the subsistence needs of one person. The other production process takes place on farms. It does not employ any seed capital, and takes sixteen hours of labor to produce *b* units of corn. Now suppose an equal distribution of seed corn. Person 1, a factory worker, takes his or her ⅓ unit of seed corn, which provides enough raw material to labor for four hours, and produces ½ *b* units of output. Persons 2 and 3 then provide person 1 with their shares of corn capital. Person 1 then works another eight hours in the factory, producing *b* units of output. Person 1 keeps ½ *b* as wages, and persons 2 and 3 divide up the rest, each taking ¼ *b* as profit. Because all corn seed in the economy is now used up, persons 2 and 3 must work as farmers for twelve hours each to obtain the other ¾ *b* units of corn they require for subsistence.

In this example there is an initial egalitarian distribution of productive resources. And there is an egalitarian result, in which all three work twelve hours and receive back *b* units of corn. Roemer correctly noted that most Marxists would find it extremely odd to term this an exploitative situation. But person 1 does engage in wage labor for persons 1 and 2 and does perform four hours of surplus labor, the fruits of which are then appropriated by persons 2 and 3. And so, according to Marx's definition of exploitation in terms of surplus labor extraction, this would mistakenly be termed as a case of exploitation. Therefore, Roemer concluded, something is wrong with Marx's definition.

Exploitation Can Occur Without Surplus Labor Extraction

Roemer provided two cases where there is exploitation without surplus labor being extracted from the exploited by the exploiter. First, he presented a model of an economy in which there is no labor market whatsoever, but in which a credit market leads to results formally isomorphic to exploitation through a labor market. He concluded that

> This analysis challenges those who believe that the process of labor exchange is *the* critical moment in the genesis of capitalist exploitation.... Exploitation can be mediated entirely through the exchange of produced commodities, and classes can exist with respect to a credit market instead of a labor market.... Capitalist exploitation is the appropriation of the labor of one class by another class because of their differential ownership or access to the [nonhuman] means of production. This can be accomplished, in principle, with or without a direct relationship between the exploiters and the exploited in the process of work.[3]

Roemer's second illustration is the phenomenon of unequal exchange. Imagine a situation in which producers are limited in their choice of production plans by their wealth, such that rich producers engage exclusively in more capital-intensive production activities and poor ones must concentrate on labor-intensive processes. They then trade the output they have produced to attain the same subsistence bundle. If certain noncontroversial background assumptions are added, it can be shown that in general poor producers work longer than is socially necessary and rich producers work less. The rich therefore can be said to exploit the poor producers. But this does not appear to be a warranted assertion on the Marxian definition of exploitation. For the exploited have not sold their wage labor to the exploiters, and the exploiters do not extract surplus labor from the exploited at the point of production.[4]

The Dispensability of the Category "Exploitation"

Roemer not only held that Marx's category of "exploitation" must be abandoned, he also believed that any emphasis on exploitation is mistaken. In Roemer's perspective what is important from a normative point of view is inequality in the distribution of productive resources: "I say [that] exploitation theory, in the general case, is misconceived. It does not provide a proper model or account of Marxian moral sentiments; the proper Marxian claim, I think, is for equality in the distribution of productive forces, not for the elimination of exploitation."[5] In some cases the existence of exploitation mirrors this sort of inequality, but in other cases it does not.

If to increase their wealth by *x* percent the wealthy are willing to increase their labor time by some *x* plus *y* percent (i.e., the cross-sectional labor supply curve is elastic with respect to wealth), then cases may result where the poor exploit the wealthy. Suppose it takes 1 unit of corn and one day of labor to produce 2 units of corn in a factory setting. Person A has 1 unit of corn, whereas person B has 3. Person A could take the 1 unit and labor for one day in the factory, and then consume 1 of the produced corn units while retaining the other for the next cycle. Person B could obtain 6 units of corn in the factory, allowing him or her to consume 3 units and retain 3 for the start of the next cycle. But suppose that person A would prefer to have ⅔ unit of corn if it did not require any labor to obtain. And suppose person B preferred to consume 3⅓ units, even if this meant having to work for four days. Then person B might borrow A's 1 unit, work four days in the factory, and produce 8 units of corn. Then, 1⅔ units could be returned to person A to repay the loan with interest. Person B then could consume 3⅓ units, and retain 3 units for the next cycle. Person A could consume ⅔ units of corn and retain 1 unit. This process can be repeated indefinitely.

Because person A never works and lives off interest ultimately stemming from person B's labor, person A is exploiting person B. But person B is far richer. Roemer asserts that what Marxists ought to care about is this inequality in the distribution of productive resources. Because the poor can exploit the wealthy, exploitation is not an accurate guide to the normatively significant matter. Marx is to be faulted not just for the particular definition of exploitation that he gave, but for making the concept central to his theory in the first place.[6]

An Outline of Marx's System

Of course every defense of Marx's theory depends on a reading of his work. Thus far the defenses proposed by Marxists have interpreted his theory in terms of the empirical social sciences.[7] This approach is not mistaken by any means. In *Capital* and elsewhere Marx made numerous and profound contributions to economics, political science, history, sociology, anthropology, and so on. However there is another dimension of his theory as well. In previous chapters I termed this the *systematic dialectical dimension* of his thought. Throughout the book I argued that this is a central component of the Hegelian legacy in Marx, as Marx took over this sort of theory from Hegel. Before evaluating Roemer's rejection of Marx's concept of exploitation from this perspective, I would like to call to mind again the main outlines of this methodology.

Marx's *Capital* can be read as a reconstruction in thought of the capitalist mode of production. A reconstruction in thought of a form of social production necessarily involves the use of categories. If it is to be comprehensive, it requires a *system* of categories. These categories do not all fall on the same theoretical level. Some categories articulate social structures that are more simple and abstract than others. For our purposes a theory can be said to follow a dialectical logic if (a) categories that articulate simple and abstract social structures are ordered prior to categories that define more complex and concrete structures and (b) each category fixes a structure that incorporates the structures presented in the prior categories and in turn is incorporated in the structures fixed by subsequent categories. In this sense early categories are principles for the derivation of later ones. This is the familiar Hegelian notion of *Aufhebung* or "sublation." This sort of categorial theory is found in Hegel's systematic writings. And however much Marx differed from Hegel in other respects, Marx's theory is a dialectical theory in this sense.

I also argued earlier that systematic dialectical logic and the search for microfoundations characteristic of analytic Marxism are compatible in principle. How are transitions from one determination to another justified within a systematic social theory? Each category defines a social form on a certain level of abstraction. If it can be shown that it is necessarily the case that there is a dominant structural tendency built into that social form leading to a more concrete social structure, then the necessity of making a transition to a category that fixes the more concrete structure in thought has been established. To maintain that such structural tendencies are necessary, one must show that within the structural parameters defined by the initial category social agents necessarily would tend to choose certain courses of action. And this means that microfoundations must be provided for dialectical transitions in the process whereby "the abstract determinations lead towards a reproduction of the concrete by way of thought."[8]

Before evaluating Roemer's criticisms from a systematic viewpoint we first must sketch the systematic ordering of socioeconomic categories proposed by Marx. Obviously there is not enough space here either to present this ordering in detail nor to defend its adequacy.[9] I shall list only those stages of the theory that are of most interest in the present context.

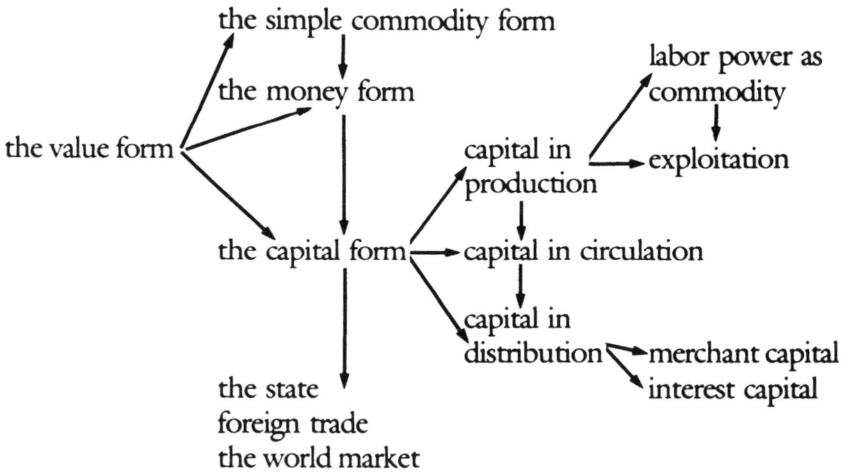

This diagram is to be read from left to right and from top to bottom. The ordering follows a dialectical logic as defined above. Each succeeding determination represents a social structure that is more complex and concrete when compared to that which preceded it, and each incorporates ("sublates") the structures that have gone before. The content of the categories most important for our purposes will be discussed in the course of evaluating Roemer's criticisms.

Replies to Roemer's Objections

"Exploitation" Cannot Stand Alone

Roemer's first objection to the Marxian notion of exploitation was that it could not stand alone. Even the most elementary comprehension of systematic dialectical theories reveals how insubstantial an objection this is. In dialectical theories *no* category can ever stand alone; *every* category receives its meaning only in terms of its systematic place within the theory as a whole.

Let us place the category "exploitation" within its systematic context. It is the second category of the capital form, directly following "labor power as commodity." The category "labor power as commodity" articulates a structure within which those who own only their labor power are free in a double sense. They are free from any ownership or control of society's productive resources, and they are free to sell themselves to those who do own or control those resources:

> For the conversion of his money into capital, therefore, the owner of money must meet in the market with the free labourer, free in the double sense, that as a free man he can dispose of his labour-power as his own commodity, and that on the other hand he has no other commodity for sale, is short of everything necessary for the realisation of his labour-power.[10]

This category serves as the proximate principle for the derivation of the category "exploitation." The latter category therefore incorporates ("sublates") the former. More precisely it fixes a structure within which the preceding distribution of productive resources is presupposed. Thus when Roemer pointed out that Marx's category of "exploitation" cannot stand on its own, that it crucially involves the separation of wage labor from the means of production, this is hardly news, to put it mildly. Roemer could present this obvious fact as a criticism of Marx only because he has overlooked that the ordering of categories in *Capital* follows a dialectical logic.

Surplus Labor Extraction Can Occur Without Exploitation

When we turn to Roemer's second objection there are two points to consider. The first, less crucial, question to ask is whether rational agents would select the arrangement Roemer described in his thought experiment. A stable equilibrium can be attained in which person 1 does not sell his or her labor power to persons 2 and 3 and does not labor in the factory the entire workday. He or she instead can work four hours in the factory with the ⅓ units of seed corn, produce ½ *b* of corn, and then walk out to the field next to the factory and labor for eight additional hours to produce the other ½ *b*. And persons 2 and 3 could do precisely the same.

At first Roemer asserts merely that the agents would be indifferent between this arrangement and the one in which persons 2 and 3 hire person 1. Then he suggested that workers who aim at minimizing the length of the workday (keeping the subsistence bundle they earn constant) might prefer to remain in the same workplace. After all, it takes time to move between factory and field.[11] However this reasoning fails to take into account that "constant labor of one uniform kind disturbs the intensity and flow of a man's animal spirits, which find recreation and delight in mere change of activity." Marx saw this as a fundamental feature of the human condition.[12] If this were built into Roemer's model, then rational agents would not select the arrangement Roemer describes as a counterexample to Marx's notion of exploitation (unless the travel time between workplaces was extremely burdensome).

This, however, is not the major problem with Roemer's counterexample. The recognition of the systematic and dialectical nature of *Capital* provides a much more substantial reason why his objection missed the mark. Roemer argued that Marx's surplus labor definition of exploitation in capitalism may lead one to assert that a nonexploitative situation is exploitative. But the thought experiment Roemer constructed to establish this thesis begins with an egalitarian distribution of productive resources. In contrast, Marx's notion of "exploitation" includes (dialectically sublates) the category "labor power as commodity." And this category refers to a fundamentally *inegalitarian* distribution of production resources. In other words, Roemer constructed a situation in which Marx's category of exploitation is by definition inapplicable and then presented its inapplicability as a great objection to that category.

Marx's theoretical aim is the reconstruction in thought of a specific social form. His claim was not that all surplus labor extraction necessarily involves exploitation. His claim rather was that the capital form necessarily involves an extraction of surplus labor that is exploitative. In Roemer's thought experiment the capital form is not operative. And so it cannot establish anything of relevance to Marx's claim.

This is connected with the question of socialist society. Roemer asserted that there is some ambiguity in Marxism here:

> Surplus value may also be produced under socialism... but the classical Marxian theory does not adequately distinguish among the different natures of surplus production.... For instance, there has been a debate about whether socialism must entail zero growth, a confusion that comes about because the classical theory of exploitation does not adequately distinguish the different property relations under capitalism and socialism.[13]

But in Marx's "Critique of the Gotha Program"[14] he unequivocally stated that in socialism the associated producers would *not* receive back the total social product. Part of that product would be allocated toward replacing, expanding, and ensuring the social means of production, toward providing for the means of social consumption, and toward aiding those unable to work.

As Hegel said, the truth is the whole. Surplus labor extraction means different things in different institutional contexts. Under socialism it does not mean what it does under capitalism. The category "exploitation" in *Capital* is introduced in the context of a systematic dialectic of the social forms that make up the capitalist mode of production. This category cannot be ripped out of the systematic context and applied to a completely different set of social forms without distorting Marx's position. And yet that is what Roemer has done.

Exploitation Can Occur Without Surplus Labor Extraction

This brings us to the third objection, the argument that the surplus labor definition of exploitation cannot account for some forms of exploitation: exploitation through credit markets and through unequal exchange. Regarding exploitation in credit markets, Roemer once again was reinventing the wheel. Marx himself was fully aware that credit mechanisms could lead to exploitation even though no exchange of labor power connects exploiter and exploited.[15] However, perhaps we can push Roemer's point a bit to formulate a more plausible objection.

Marx claimed that exploitation through credit markets is a secondary form of exploitation. As such it must come fairly late in the categorial ordering. In the discussion of interest-bearing capital and merchant capital in volume 3 of *Capital* we read that

> It is still more irrelevant to drag the lending of houses, etc. for individual use into this discussion. That the working-class is also swindled in this form, and to an enormous extent, is self-evident; but... This is secondary exploitation, which runs parallel to the primary exploitation process taking place in the production process itself.[16]

Marx thus asserts that exploitation of wage labor is more essential than exploitation through credit mechanisms. Perhaps Roemer's criticism could be revised to call into question this ordering. Roemer has shown that the two forms of exploitation are formally isomorphic. Why then should one form of exploitation be given priority over the other?

The problem with this version of the objection is that it too is based on a misunderstanding of Marx's theoretical project. Exploitation within the creditor-debtor social relation is a feature of many sorts of social systems, including those of the ancient feudal periods as well as modern capitalism. This cannot be said of exploitation within the social relation connecting the buyers and the sellers of labor power. This is unique to capitalism. Hence if the theoretical project is a systematic reconstruction in thought of the fundamental determination of a *specific* form of social production, the capital form, then there is a substantial reason to grant one sort of exploitation a systematic priority, even if from a formal standpoint the two are isomorphic.

Turning to unequal exchange, here too Roemer's claim to have discovered a type of exploitation that Marx did not or could not recognize simply does not wash. Marx was well aware that trade between countries with capital-intensive technologies and poorer countries with labor-intensive production facilities would result in the exploitation of the less developed countries, even if no purchase or sale of labor power connects the two.[17]

If Roemer had said instead that Marx is to be faulted for not granting this form of exploitation equal primacy with the exploitation stemming from the capital-wage labor relation, then once again the objection would have been more plausible. For there is a formal isomorphism between the two types of exploitation. But once again an exclusive stress on formal matters prevents an understanding of Marx's theory on its own terms. The relation between capital and wage labor is simpler and more abstract than the social relationship connecting the two national entities. The latter includes the former, while adding to it further determinations. Hence in a dialectic of categories moving from the simple and more abstract to the more complex and concrete, there are systematic reasons for the former preceding the latter. We should remember that the three volumes of *Capital* are only a fragment of Marx's complete system. After the theoretical reconstruction of capital in production, circulation, and distribution, Marx anticipated three yet more concrete and complex stages of his theory: the state, foreign trade, and the world market.[18] Had Marx lived to complete his project, the discussion of unequal exchange would have found its proper systematic context in volume 5, the book on foreign trade.

The Dispensability of the Category "Exploitation"

From the standpoint of dialectical logic Roemer's fourth objection is by far the most powerful. For it can be reformulated in terms that strike to the heart of the claim that *Capital* presents a strict dialectic of economic categories. When Roemer argued that those who are poor in productive resources can exploit those who are wealthy, this calls into question the cogency of Marx's systematic progression. There now does not seem to be any theoretical necessity for the move from a category defining a structural inequality in the distribution of productive resources to the category of "exploitation." If a dialectical transition is not warranted here, then Marx's attempt to reconstruct the capitalist mode of production in a systematic fashion would have to be judged a failure.

Before drawing such a drastic conclusion, however, we should recall that the category preceding "exploitation" in Marx's system is not "inequality in the distribution of productive resources." It is "labor power as a commodity," which is a very specific sort of inequality. It is an inequality in which one class of social agents does not have access to the means of production and thus is structurally coerced to sell its labor power to another class of social agents. In the thought-experiment Roemer constructed to show why exploitation should be downplayed, person A has fewer productive resources than person B. *But person A still has sufficient resources to provide for his or her own subsistence*. This structural feature of the story completely undermines its usefulness for an evaluation of Marx's category of exploitation.

An example may clarify this point. Imagine a relatively large capitalist firm whose extremely rich managers have purchased it through a leveraged buyout. Investors possessing relatively small amounts of capital then purchase shares in the firm. Assume further that the managers are hard-working while the investors are coupon clippers, able to live off the dividends sent to them. In Roemer's sense of the term the (capitalist) investors therefore "exploit" the (capitalist) managers. Of course one can define terms however one wishes. But it should be clear that this usage of *exploitation* has absolutely nothing to do with how Marx employed the term. It is not any old inequality in the distribution of productive resources that concerned Marx, but inequalities that define interclass relations. And it was not any old transfers of surplus labor that interested Marx, but transfers that define interclass relations.

Roemer's mastery of the techniques for constructing formal models is most impressive. But any attempt to criticize Marx (or defend him, for that matter) that does not come to terms with dialectical logic is doomed to fail. The utter failure of Roemer to grasp Marx's theory of exploitation shows that analytical Marxists still have a thing or two to learn from Lenin: "It is impossible to completely understand Marx's *Capital*, and especially its first chapter, without having thoroughly studied and understood the *whole* of Hegel's *Logic*."[19]

VIII

The Critique of Marxism in Baudrillard's Late Writings

The politics of postmodernism is a variant of the politics of post-Marxism. At least most of the figures associated with the postmodernist movement have declared that they are "beyond" Marx in some fundamental fashion. This is certainly the case for Jean Baudrillard.[1] He first presented his case against Marxism in his early work, *The Mirror of Production*.[2] In this final chapter I examine some of the major objections to Marxism formulated in Baudrillard's later writings. First, however, a brief summary of relevant portions of the Marxist position must be given. These all involve central aspects of Marx's dialectical social theory.

1. Both Hegel and Marx interpret sociopolitical reality in terms of a dialectic between the moments of universality, particularity, and individuality. For Marx, "capital" is the principle of universality operating in generalized commodity exchange.

2. Marx's social theory investigated the degree to which the moments of universality, particularity, and individuality are reconciled within material modes of production. This is opposed to Hegel's examination, which gave priority to the cultural and political sphere.

3. For Hegel the poles of universality, particularity and individuality are reconciled in principle in the modern capitalist state. In this sense for Hegel the real has become rational. For Marx, in contrast, capital is an alien form of universality. It involves the exploitation of particular classes and does not allow true individuality to flourish. Therefore for

Marx the real is not rational. However there are structural contradictions in reality that create the objective possibility of a transition to a social order where the universal (i.e., the community as a whole), particular groups within the community, and individuals truly can be reconciled. This is a dialectic of history (as opposed to *systematic* dialectic, a distinct sort of dialectical theory). The most basic contradiction is between the class with a fundamental interest in maintaining the given institutional framework and the class with a fundamental interest in attaining a new set of institutions. The former class benefits from the labor of others, whereas the latter class is both exploited at the point of production and enjoys a precarious and incomplete satisfaction of its needs. All this presupposes both that there is a truth regarding such things as human needs and that in principle we can discover that truth.

4. According to Marx, the power of the alien form of capital can begin to be dissolved through an unmasking of illusions generated in social processes. This is analogous to the way in Hegel's account Greek comedy unmasked illusions generated in Greek tragedy. This process of unmasking is termed *ideology critique* in the Marxist tradition.[3]

5. Ideology critique by itself, however, is not sufficient. Abolishing alien powers requires practical activity. In a manner that goes completely beyond Hegel Marxism privileges some forms of activity. Praxis devoted to the resolution of social contradictions in a direction favorable to the interests of the exploited furthers the struggle to attain the next stage in the dialectic of history. In the present historical context, this theoretical schema orients and justifies revolutionary struggles to replace capitalism with socialism.

Baudrillard's Case Against Marxism

For Baudrillard all of the preceding is hopelessly out of date. The Marxist account utterly fails to appreciate the specificity of our postmodern condition. Baudrillard rejected each of the five points. In doing so he abandoned completely dialectical social theory.

Beyond the Dialectic of Universality, Particularity, and Individuality

In Baudrillard's view today we live in the epoch of simulation. The real event has been replaced by the simulacra of a real event, simulacra that multiply themselves endlessly in all directions. The world we dwell in is dominated by images that pretend to depict a reality but that depict only themselves. When we come to see "reality" in terms of these images, then these images have become our reality. But it is a reality more real than reality itself, a hyperreality that "substitutes signs of the real for the real itself."[4]

In this new epoch any dialectic connecting universal, particular, and individual is ruled out. On the one side, the universal is dissolved ("The universal no longer exists."[5]). Specifically, "capital" no longer functions as a universal once we are within "the hyperreal, which no longer has anything to do with either capital or the social."[6] On the other side the individual is dissolved into "the anonymous and perfectly undifferentiated individual, the term substitutable for any other... the end products of the social, of a now globalised abstract society."[7] A world dissolved into undifferentiated individuals has no room for a dialectic between the real and the rational. "There is no longer any critical and speculative distance between the real and the rational.... Neither realised nor idealised: but hyperrealized."[8]

Beyond the Productivist Paradigm

For Baudrillard "Marxism's assumption in its purest form" is "productivity regarded as a discourse of total reference."[9] Marx's concern with production simply reflected that of nineteenth century capitalism itself, which focused on production with a maniacal obsession. However Baudrillard held that a fundamental shift has occurred since Marx's day. The rupture took place when the system developed to the point where so much could be produced that consumers had to be molded so that they would absorb ever more products. We are now in a radically new period from that described by Marx, one in which the old language of capitalism has been put out of play:

> Everything changes with the precession of the production of demand before that of goods. Their logical relationship [between production and consumption] is broken, and we move into a totally different order, which is no longer that of either production, or consumption, but that of the simulation of both, thanks to the inversion of the process.[10]

Another way of putting the reason why a theory of modes of production is now outmoded is that the molding of consumers takes place through cultural images. In other words, there is now a complete interpenetration of the cultural realm and the realm of production. Things have moved to the point where there no longer are mere means of production. "We live everywhere already in an 'esthetic' hallucination of reality."[11]

The Marxist concern with production extends to the production of theory, the production of meanings that make sense of the world. Here Baudrillard claimed that Marxism had fallen into a trap set by capitalism. Ironically it provided a support for the very system it intended to undermine, for "It is the production of this demand for meaning which has become crucial for the system,"[12] even if this is but the simulation of a production of meaning.

Beyond Needs; Beyond Truth

Marxist discourse essentially involves truth claims that are supposedly grounded by objectively existing referents. In specific, the theory of needs was a crucial component of Marx's critique of capitalism. "Unmet social needs" provided a naturally existing reference point in terms of which the failures of capitalism could be objectively measured. In this manner the truth of the critique could be grounded. Postmodern thinkers, however, reject the notion that there is some transcendental referent for the signs that we use, grounding the truth of our assertions. Baudrillard spoke of the "liquidation of all referentials."[13] "Needs," for example, are not naturalistically given and thus cannot ground the truth of Marxist discourse.

Beyond Ideology

The concept of ideology implies that some reality has been falsely presented. The concept of ideology critique implies that it is possible to present the truth of that reality. If reality has been replaced by hyperreality and if the notion of truth must be abandoned along with that of reference, then it follows at once that the concepts of ideology and ideology critique cannot be retained. Baudrillard did not shy away from drawing this conclusion. Today, "It is no longer a question of the false representation of reality (ideology), but of concealing the fact that the real is no longer real."[14] Here too Marxism must be rejected, for "It is always a false problem to want to restore the truth beneath the simulacrum."[15]

Beyond Revolution

From all that has been said thus far it follows that the project of revolutionary action oriented by the rational understanding of dialectical social reality must be completely abandoned. Any attempt to escape from the simulations of hyperreality only further entraps us in it. Where does this leave us? Baudrillard seemed to propose two answers. One suggestion is that a radical project today does not attempt to struggle against the ceaseless production of hyperreality. Instead the radical today is like a judo master who accepts the force thrown against her, and who even reinforces that force, thereby throwing it off. Baudrillard's advice to us is to amplify the hyperreality around us, to give in to its fascination, rather than to attempt to resist it. He terms this hyperconformism: "The strategic resistance is that of... the hyperconformist simulation of the very mechanisms of the system, which is a form of refusal and of non-reception."[16] This amplification may then lead to the "implosion" of the hyperreality, to a catastrophe whose dimensions cannot be predicted or imagined at this point. Anything short of this implosion does not count as a radical act in the present context; anything else would not go to the root of the matter.

A second option seems to involve a more active form of resistence. It involves a "challenge" to the production of hyperreality:

> Challenge is the opposite of *dialogue*: it creates a nondialectic, ineluctable space. It is neither a means nor an end: it opposes its own space to political space. It knows neither middle-range nor long-term; its only term is the immediacy of a response or of death. Everything linear, including history, has an end; challenge alone is without end since it is indefinitely reversible.[17]

Challenge in this sense counts as the purest form of defiance, for "Defiance always comes from that which has no meaning, no name, no identity — it is a defiance of meaning, or power, of truth."[18]

For Baudrillard the greatest moments of working-class rebellion were not the goal-directed attempts to seize state power, but those revolts that fit this notion of challenge. Here too what was sought was an "implosion," not a revolution:

> The *real* history of class struggle... [its] only moments were those when the dominated class fought on the basis of its self-denial "as such," on the

> basis of the sole fact that it amounted to nothing. . . . When the class itself, or a faction of it, prefers to act as a radical non-class, i.e. to act out its own death right away within the explosive structure of capital, when it chooses to implode suddenly instead of seeking political expansion and class hegemony. . . . The secret of the void lies here, in the incalculable force of the implosion (contrary to our imaginary concept of revolutionary explosion).[19]

But for Baudrillard even this seems to be a matter of the past. The socialist project of a class-based revolution is ruled out today because in a world of hyperreality there cannot be any real classes to serve as revolutionary agents. From this perspective the very project of socialism is dissolved: "The social will never have had time to lead to socialism, it will have been short-circuited by the hypersocial, by the hyperreality of the social."[20] In a world of undifferentiated individuals "the concept of class will have dissolved . . . into some parodic, extended double, like 'the mass of workers' or simply into a retrospective of the proletariat."[21]

Evaluation of Baudrillard's Arguments

How ought we evaluate Baudrillard's writings? In a certain sense Baudrillard has undercut all possibility of objecting to his position by insisting that he did not have a position. He has insisted that he was not in the least interested in presenting truth claims. His objective instead was to use the language of thought to make himself and his readers "dizzy" with the experience: "My way is to make ideas appear, but as soon as they appear I immediately try to make them disappear . . . nothing remains but a sense of dizziness, with which you can't do anything."[22] However certainly more is going on in his writings than the attempt to evoke that one emotion. Baudrillard's writings clearly also are meant to *persuade* us of various things, from the bankruptcy of Marxism to the characteristics of the postmodern world. This implies, however, that it is legitimate to raise the question whether Baudrillard's points are persuasive.

My thesis is that there is a built-in tension between the project of making the reader experience dizziness and the project of persuading the reader of the correctness of a given interpretation. A plausible case for the correctness of a specific insight generally involves things such as spelling out carefully the implications of accepting the insight, discussing the range of cases to which it applies and the range to which it does not apply, considering alternative insights that attempt to account for the same range, and so on. In contrast intellectual dizziness is most reliably evoked when one begins with a specific insight and then wildly extrapolates to the most extreme thesis that could possibly be connected to that insight. Given the obvious divergence in both method and purpose of the two projects, it would be most unlikely for a single author to combine the two successfully. As far as Baudrillard is concerned, there can be no doubt that his writings successfully evoke dizziness in the reader. However his success in presenting us with reasons to regard his critique of Marxism as plausible is much more doubtful. With this thesis in mind we can go through Baudrillard's key claims in turn.

Beyond the Dialectic of Universality, Particularity, and Individuality?

All three dialectical moments can be found in Baudrillard, although not in the form presented by Marx. The moment of individuality certainly is present in his thought, even if in the debased form of "the anonymous and perfectly undifferentiated individual."[23] And the various codes or models repeated over and over in the production of hyperreality form a moment of particularity. At first it may appear that this is all that there is. Baudrillard wrote that "The universal no longer exists, there is nothing left but a singularity which can take on the aspect of totality."[24] But this is not quite right. It turns out that for Baudrillard, no less than for Marx, the form of capital was an alien universal above individuals. If anything, capital for Baudrillard was even more of a universal than for Marx. Its scope extends to the innermost depths of our existence:

> This compulsion toward liquidity, flow, and an accelerated circulation of what is psychic, sexual, or pertaining to the body is the exact replica of the force which rules market value: capital must circulate; gravity and any fixed point must disappear; the chain of investments and reinvestments must never stop; value must radiate endlessly and in every direction. This is the form itself which the current realization of value takes. It is the form of capital, and sexuality as a catchword and a *model* is the way it appears at the level of bodies.... It is capital which gives birth in the same movement to the energetic of labor power and to the body we dream of today as the locus of desire and the unconscious.... To rediscover in the secret of bodies an unbound 'libidinal' energy which would be opposed to the bound energy of productive bodies, and to rediscover a phantasmal and instinctual truth of the body in desire, is still only to unearth the psychic metaphor of capital.[25]

Baudrillard thus cannot consistently claim that his thought did not involve the abstract categories of universal, particularity, and individual.

His claim that "The universal no longer exists" is a wild extrapolation from the fact that the alien universal of capital is more extensive and intensive in its scope than ever before.

Turning to more concrete matters, are there objective dialectical tendencies (in the historical, as opposed to the systematic, sense) in the present configuration for Baudrillard? At first it might seem as if this question, of such central importance to Marx, is no longer of relevance. After all, Baudrillard has written that "dialectical polarity no longer exists."[26] But a closer look at Baudrillard's position reveals that this cannot be maintained. On the one hand, he pointed to the endless and impersonal production of a meaningless hyperreality. On the other, there is the "silent majority" that dwells in this hyperreality. In his view the production of hyperreality generates the preconditions for an ironic hyperconformism in the silent majority or for a challenge and defiance of the present order. Either way Baudrillard has argued in effect that there is a "dialectical polarity" between hyperreality and the silent majority. From this he derived an objective structural tendency toward what he termed *implosion*. Like it or not, with this he in effect has formulated a hypothesis regarding a dialectical development. Whatever the plausibility of this scenario, it is the unfolding of a historical dialectic. Baudrillard has made a wild extrapolation from the fact that the dialectic he sketched is quite different from other accounts to the conclusion that the very category of dialectical tendencies must be abandoned.

Beyond Production?

Baudrillard began with an interesting insight. Capitalism has become so productive that the danger of producing commodities that are not absorbed by the market is ever present. This means that great effort continually must be made to create demand for products. When products are cultural signs the demand for them will not be limited by any functional use those products may have. In this sense there is no longer (if there ever was) any sphere of production separate from the sphere of culture.[27]

From this observation Baudrillard extrapolated to the claims that any attempt to consider production independent of culture is mistaken and that any attempt by critics of capitalism to produce cultural meanings supports the very system they meant to oppose. Neither of these claims withstands scrutiny.

Production and culture certainly are mediated together, but this does not necessarily imply that they are fused. It may be the case that they are united-in-difference. If so, it would be legitimate to consider production apart from culture, as long as one realizes that the mediation of the two spheres must be comprehended if the level of concretion is to be obtained.

The proof that the two spheres are distinguishable in their unity comes from the fact that some things can be comprehended only if production is considered in abstraction from its connection to culture. The hyperreality of which Baudrillard spoke is itself produced. Even if it were the case that the production of images is now more crucial to the present stage of capital than the production of material products, we cannot extrapolate from this to the conclusion that the question of the ownership and control of the means of production is not of crucial significance.

A tremendous concentration of capital resides in the ownership and control of the means of producing messages. Robert Maxwell and Rupert Murdoch have created global media empires that spread through book, magazine, and newspaper publishing; TV station ownership; TV program planning; cable TV network ownership; satellite TV distribution; and electronic hardware production. Time and Warners have merged into a media conglomerate with revenues of $10 billion a year. The next Madonna wannabe will be signed by Warners, given a HBO special, reviewed in Time, and appear on the cover of People in a hyperreal blitz — all as a result of a decision made by headquarters in New York. Surely a consideration of such matters cannot be avoided if we wish to understand the dynamics of our hyperreal postmodern world. Baudrillard cannot possibly provide any sort of argument that his thought leads us beyond Marx's concern with the ownership and control of the means of production. Marxism has not suddenly become outdated with the rise of the electronic mass media. The age of hyperreality confirms Marx's essential insight that the concentration and centralization of control of the means of production is inherent in the logic of capital and that this generates alien social forces standing above the members of society.[28]

Turning to the other issue to be considered here, Baudrillard began with a very plausible insight into the connection of capitalism and the production of meanings. He pointed out that the capitalist order must continually produce meanings if for no other reason than to hide how much the workings of this order in fact have produced generalized meaninglessness. From this insight, however, he went on to extrapolate wildly to the thesis that *any* production of meanings serves the interests of capitalism, those that reject the logic of capitalism no less than those that accept that logic: "All that capital asks of us is to receive it as rational or to combat it in the name of rationality, to receive it as moral or to combat it in the name of morality."[29] In specific he claims that Marxism's commitment to produce theories that make sense of the social world is just another form of the production of meanings by means of which capitalism continues.

With one wave of his magisterial hand Baudrillard ruled out there being *any* possibility whatsoever that Marxist accounts of the social world might contribute to a counterhegemony that seriously threatens the stability of the capitalist order. One need not assert that the meanings produced by Marxist theory presently are about to have this effect to dismiss Baudrillard's extrapolation. He has not presented any reasons to believe that it is impossible in principle that they might *ever* have this effect.

Beyond Needs and Truth?

Baudrillard was quite correct to insist that all needs are socially and culturally defined. But he was mistaken if he believed that Marx was not aware of this.[30] More important, he was wrong when he extrapolated from this to the conclusion that needs are *solely* a matter of codes, systems of signifiers that refer to no referent. In its own way, the view that states that human needs have no natural or biological basis is as one-sided — and therefore false — as the sociobiology position that ignores the historical and cultural component of our nature. Rather than developing this point, however, I would like to concentrate on Baudrillard's more general claim.[31] The denial that we can say anything true about the nature of our needs is just a specific case of a general rejection of the referent, a rejection of our being able to formulate truth claims regarding the signified in language.

At this point it would seem that Baudrillard was yet another victim of the old trap Aristotle set for the skeptics. A writer attempting to persuade us of the correctness of his or her views cannot consistently claim that the question of correctness is now irrelevant in our postmodern age. For this reason someone like Habermas, who recognized that validity claims are built into our speech, formulated a more plausible view than the French postmodernists who denied it.[32] However this point does not consider Baudrillard's case on it own terms. A more immanent critique can be given by considering some of the examples Baudrilllard discussed.

Baudrillard had a very plausible insight into the Watergate saga of the Nixon era. The *Washington Post* employed precisely the same undercover methods in breaking the story as the Nixon administration employed in planning the initial break-ins. Also, the source for the *Post*'s stories, "Deep Throat," may well have been someone within the Nixon administration itself. All of this is interesting enough. But at this point Baudrillard headed for the stratosphere and extrapolated from the fact that in this case we may never know the truth of the matter to the conclusion that the very category of "truth" must be abandoned.[33] Or take another of Baudrillard's cases. In the Franco years Franco ordered the public execution of some Basque nationalists. Baudrillard pointed out that this was Franco's gift to Western Europe. Western Europe could piously complain about Franco, thereby indulging in pompous and pointless self-congratulations regarding its own liberalism. And this response in turn was Western Europe's gift to Franco. The attacks on Spain allowed him to solidify his own rule by appealing to Spanish national unity. It certainly is true that in this complex web it is hard to distinguish posturing from the facts of the matter. But Baudrillard derived a much stronger conclusion: "Where is the truth in all that, when such collusions admirably knit together without their authors ever knowing it?"[34] This implies that the category "truth" would have validity only if states of affairs corresponded to the subjective intentions of the social actors who brought them about. This surely is a wild extrapolation. Baudrillard himself has illuminated what the facts of the matter probably were. He himself has captured at least an essential part of the truth of this situation, and so he is hardly in a position to claim that this sort of situation undermines the category of truth.

Anyone deriving this conclusion from the case being considered ought to feel dizzy. But anyone attempting to reject on these grounds a theory such as Marx's that makes truth claims ought to think twice.

Beyond Ideology?

Marx's category of ideology depends on there being a underlying reality that has been masked. In the age of hyperreality, however, Baudrillard insisted that this cannot be the case. When it comes to the question of social reality, there is no doubt that Baudrillard once again began with an important insight. Baudrillard's notion of simulacrum tremendously illuminated our contemporary fate. An Italian girl from Michigan with a fairly ordinary voice has become an icon because of her sophisticated manipulation of the signs of sexuality in countless[35] MTV videos. The producers of colored sugarwater have built vast empires by associating that sugarwater with the signs of youth in endlessly repeated commercials. In both cases these signs do not refer back to the commodity in question; they refer to nothing at all. And yet they are more real than real, hyperreal.

Baudrillard was at his best when he showed how contemporary politics is also nothing but a series of meaningless simulations. "Propaganda and advertising fuse in the same marketing and merchandising of objects and ideologies."[36] A better description of our Redempubocratic system could not be given than his: "Simulation of opposition between two parties, absorption of their respective objectives, reversibility of the entire discourse one into the other."[37] Politics too has been taken over by the hyperreal. Consider the manner in which Bush wrapped himself in the American flag. What did this signify? To what did it refer? Obviously it had no connection whatsoever to Bush's record as Texas oil millionaire, CIA director, or Vice-President, little of which had anything to do with the values most of the U.S. electorate associates with the flag. There was no reality to which his employment of the flag as sign referred, and yet the employment of the flag as sign had a reality of its own. In fact it too was more real than real; it was hyperreal. Or consider the Willie Horton ads. These ads functioned as signs that were clearly designed to be perceived as referring to hoards of black rapists treated leniently by liberal administrators. But the social effect of these ads, these signifiers, had nothing whatsoever to do with the question whether there was any real signified to which they referred. The only thing that mattered was that they were taken to refer to the real. In this sense the ads took on a power that made them more than real. They also created a hyperreality.

We are surrounded by signs that have profound effects in the social world without referring to anything real. In forcing us to confront this, Baudrillard made a significant contribution to contemporary social theory. But he was not content to leaves things there. Instead he pushed the wild extrapolation button and came up with the thesis that we have entered the epoch of the simulacrum. The "decisive turning point" that marks our age is "the transition from signs which dissimulate something to signs which dissimulate that there is nothing."[38]

This induces the sought-for dizziness, but it does so at the cost of coherence. To know that Bush's appeal to the flag created a hyperreality rather than referring to anything real about Bush, one must *already* know that *in reality* Bush's career reflects a commitment to values quite different from those most of the populace associate with the flag. To know that Willie Horton ads created a hyperreality rather than referring to anything real in the social world, one must *already* know that *in reality* the myth of the black rapist is just that, a myth,[39] and that *in reality* the U.S. legal system is guilty of massive and systematic discrimination against black men. The category of hyperreality thus cannot be a *replacement* for the concept of reality as Baudrillard held. We must presuppose the validity of the latter term to determine instances where the former term is exemplified.

The signs around us do not hide from us that there is nothing; they hide from us that Madonna's poses oversimplify human sexuality, that Pepsi is colored sugarwater, that Bush's campaign was hypocritical and racist. These signs distort and mask underlying reality, a reality that thought in principle can appropriate, as many of Baudrillard's own writings show.[40] This implies that the age of simulacra is another stage *within* the age of ideology and not some radically new epoch where the Marxist concept of ideology has become irrelevant.

Beyond Revolution?

Two points can be considered under this heading: did Baudrillard present a compelling case against the project of revolutionary class struggle and did he present an acceptable alternative?

First, we have seen that Baudrillard held that the idea of a revolution furthering the interests of the working classes is senseless today. His argument was that in an age of hyperreality the very concept of class becomes a "parody," a "retrospective simulation." However Baudrillard himself granted that there is exploitation in the present order. This seems to imply that we are able to distinguish the exploiting classes from those exploited without resorting to parody or simulation. Baudrillard seemed to acknowledge this. However he simply denied its interest: "Exploiters and exploited do in fact exist, they are on different sides because there is no reversibility in production, which is precisely the point: nothing essential happens at that level."[41]

Of course this argument depends entirely on the unstated premise that "reversibility" is the distinguishing characteristic of what is "essential." Why should one grant this premise? Baudrillard did not attempt to argue for it in any way. It is true that many significant social relations are "reversible"; it often is possible to observe the observer, to dominate the dominating, and so on. But why extrapolate from this to the claim that "nothing essential happens" unless there is reversibility? Is the essentiality of a phenomenon not a function of its importance within a given social order?

At any rate, Baudrillard did not really claim that there are no classes, only that class struggle is useless. He held that no dialectic within the present epoch could possibly point to socialism being on the historical agenda. "Once capital itself has become its own myth, or rather an interminable machine, aleatory, something like a *social genetic code*, it no longer leaves any room for a planned reversal; and this is its true violence."[42]

Arguments for the inevitable success of socialism are surely suspect. But are arguments for the inevitability of the failure of socialism any less suspect? Baudrillard's case for the thesis that capital "no longer leaves any room for a planned reversal" appeals to the fact that in the industrialized West the labor union apparatus has been integrated into the bourgeois order. "Strikes...are incorporated like obsolescence in objects, like crisis in production....There is no longer any strikes or work, but...scenodrama (not to say melodrama) of production, collective dramaturgy upon the empty stage of the social."[43]

The wild extrapolation here is transparent. From the present relative passivity of the labor movement Baudrillard jumped to the conclusion that all capital-wage labor confrontations in principle can never be more than the mere simulation of conflict. He completely ruled out in principle any possibility of there ever being dissident movements within the labor movement that successfully unite workers with consumers, women, racially oppressed groups, environmental activists, and so forth in a common struggle against capital. He completely ruled out in principle the possibility of a dynamic unfolding of this struggle to the point where capital's control of investment decisions is seriously called into question. He made a wild extrapolation from the fact that these things are not on the agenda today to the conclusion that in principle they cannot ever occur. To say that he failed to provide any plausible arguments for such a strong position is to put things far too mildly.

Second, Baudrillard's alternatives to organized struggle against capital are hyperconformism and defiance. Examples of the former range from yuppies who accumulate the latest electronic gadgets with the proper demeanor of hip irony, to the crack dealing B-Boys whose obsession with designer labels and BMWs simulates the hypermaterialism of the very system that has destroyed their communities. Rampant hyperconformism of this sort very well may lead the system to implode, from the waste, environmental damage, and community disintegration imposed by hyperconsumerism. The only problem is that by the time this implosion occurs it may be too late for the human species to pick up the pieces.

Baudrillard's cryptoexistentialist odes to defiance perhaps present a more attractive option; however, these odes romanticize defeat. They honor the memory of rebels not for the heroism exemplified in their defeats and not for the lessons that can be learned from such defeats. It is the defeats themselves that meet with Baudrillard's approval, the fact that the rebels were "acting out [their] own death right away . . . instead of seeking political expansion and class hegemony." This form of implosion is like fireworks that brilliantly illuminate the landscape when they go off, only to dissolve at once, leaving everything immersed in darkness as before. And this form of implosion is an option for suicide. In my view neither of Baudrillard's proposals provides a satisfactory alternative to revolutionary Marxism. I conclude that Baudrillard's postmodernism — along with the neo-Kantianism of Colletti and the analytical Marxism of Elster and Roemer — fails to present a compelling case against dialectical social theory.

Notes

Introduction

1. A number of other significant issues connected with dialectical social theory could be explored. One thing is the manner in which dialectical social theory was modified by "Western Marxists" such as Lukacs, Adorno, and Sartre. Another is the appeal to dialectics made in the traditional doctrines of the Communist Parties of the USSR, China and elsewhere. Contemporary attempts to approach psychoanalysis and feminism from a dialectical perspective provide a third area of interest. (Balbus's *Marxism and Domination* and Roger Gottlieb's *History and Subjectivity* can be mentioned in this context.) No doubt, other topics could be examined under the general topic of dialectical social theory. However I shall confine my remarks here to the two issues mentioned.

2. V.I. Lenin, *Collected Works*, vol. 38, p. 180.

3. The best known, of course, is Alexander Kojève's *Introduction to the Reading of Hegel: Lectures on the Phenomenology of Spirit*.

4. In *Dialectics of Labour*, Chris Arthur has argued that Marx was probably not as influenced by the Master-Slave dialectic as commentators have supposed.

5. For our purposes *Post-Marxism* can be defined as the view that Marx's description of nineteenth century capitalism may have been valid in his day, but no longer applies.

6. The fact that so many Marxists and post-Marxists have rejected dialectical social theory no doubt tells us something about the contemporary intellectual scene. Dialectics, in both its systematic and historical variants, is a method for

comprehending dynamic processes. The stagnation (and later collapse) of Stalinism, the retreat of the Left in the West, and the general failure of Third World movements to institute either development or democracy have undermined the belief that radical change is possible. Hence theorists have turned to approaches that are more static and ahistorical: neo-Kantianism, game theory, the evocation of simulacra. Rather than pursue this sort of sociological investigation, however, I want to concentrate on the philosophical arguments given for a rejection of dialectical social theory.

7. Perhaps the most glaring omission from this list of critics is Althusser. However, his arguments against dialectical social theory do not appear to be as influential today as those of Colletti, analytical Marxists, and postmodernists. See Ted Benton's *The Rise and Fall of Structural Marxism*.

8. I discuss two recent contributions to historical dialectics in "Two Theories of Historical Materialism: G.A. Cohen and Jürgen Habermas, Chapter IV" of my earlier work *The Role of Ethics in Social Theory*. An excellent account of historical dialectics in the Marxist tradition can be found in Joseph McCarney's *Marxism and the Crisis of Social Theory*.

I
Hegel's Theory of the Syllogism and Its Relevance for Marxism

1. Of course, this assertion is denied by contemporary poststructuralists and postmodernists. Because both Hegel and Marx accepted it, however, this issue need not be pursued here. I shall return to it in the discussion of Baudrillard in the final chapter.

2. My reading of Hegel has been influenced by the work of Klaus Hartmann. See his article, "Hegel: A Non-Metaphysical View," as well as the anthology he edited, *Die Ontologische Option*. In the United States this interpretation of Hegel has been developed by Terry Pinkard in "The Logic of Hegel's *Logic*" and *Hegel's Dialectic*; and by Alan White in his *Absolute Knowledge: Hegel and the Problem of Metaphysics*. In Chapter I of my *The Logic of Marx's Capital* I present my version of this reading in more detail.

3. See *Hegel's Logic* (encyclopedia version), p. 257.

4. This brings us to the culmination of the *Logic* as a whole. The only chapter that follows the chapters on "syllogism-object" is "Absolute Spirit." But this chapter discusses the methodology used in the *Logic*. It does not introduce any new determination into the theory.

5. *I-P-U*, *P-I-U*, and *I-U-P*, of course, are the three traditional figures of the Aristotelian theory of the syllogism. In their most abstract interpretation these three figures make up the Syllogism of Existence. On the next higher level, the Syllogism of Reflection, the same three figures are given a more adequate inter-

pretation in the Syllogism of Allness, the Syllogism of Induction, and the Syllogism of Analogy. A yet more concrete and complex interpretation of them comes with the Categorical Syllogism, the Hypothetical Syllogism, and the Disjunctive Syllogism. Taken together these three figures make up the Syllogism of Necessity. Finally, the Syllogism of Existence, the Syllogism of Reflection, and the Syllogism of Necessity themselves are interpreted in terms of the *I-P-U*, *P-I-U*, and *I-U-P* figures writ large, respectively. The details of this ordering do not concern us here. What is important to note is Hegel's insistence that on any level each of the three must be mediated with the other two if an adequate account is to be given. (Hegel also tacks on the Mathematical Syllogism at the end of the section on the Syllogism of Existence, more to include what he took to be the basic axiom of mathematics than anything else.)

6. "In the consummation of the syllogism . . . the distinction of mediating and mediated has disappeared. That which is mediated is itself an essential moment of what mediates it, and each moment appears as the totality of what is mediated." *Hegel's Science of Logic*, p. 703.

7. On the one hand, "the true result that emerges . . . is that the middle is not an individual Notion determined but the totality of them all" (ibid., p. 684). On the other hand, "the extreme also shall be posited as this *totality* which initially the middle term is" (ibid., p. 696).

8. Ibid., p. 664.

9. Ibid., p. 669.

10. "The mediating element is the objective nature of the thing" (ibid., p. 666).

11. *Hegel's Logic*, pp. 264-65. Emphasis added to last sentence.

12. In many cases representatives of the capitalist class will hold central positions in the state apparatus. In these cases, it is quite clear that the state is not a neutral institution capturing a moment of universality. However, even when representatives of the capitalist class do not control the state directly, state officials will still tend to orient their policies toward the interests of capital. There are two reasons for this. First, state officials require revenues for their projects. Because state revenues in a capitalist society generally are a function of capital accumulation, it is in the self-interest of state officials to further that accumulation. Second, if state officials did go against the perceived interests of capital in a significant fashion, this would set off an investment strike. If not addressed, such a capital strike could push the socioeconomic order into deep crisis. This in effect grants the holders of capital an ultimate veto power over state legislation. None of this is meant to imply that state-mandated reforms against the perceived interests of capital cannot be won through struggle. However, as long as the economy remains capitalist the scope of these reforms will be limited and once attained they will remain precarious.

13. See *Hegel's Philosophy of Right*, pp. 131 ff.

14. "It is necessary to help the masses in the process of daily struggle to find the bridge between present demands and the socialist programme of revolution. This bridge should include a system of *transitional demands*, starting from today's conditions and today's consciousness of wide layers of the working class and unalterably leading to one final conclusion: the conquest of power by the proletariat" (Trotsky, *The Death Agony of Capitalism*, p. 183). Examples mentioned by Trotsky include a sliding scale that ties wages to price increases and the demand that firms open their books to their workers. These demands arise in the context of the capital-wage labor relation. It is important to note that other sorts of transitional demands arise in different contexts, such as the demand that all social costs of production be taken into account, that militarism be overcome, and so on. This is crucial for the next section of this chapter.

15. Jürgen Habermas defends this view in volume 2 of his *Theorie des kommunikativen Handelns*. For a detailed critique of Habermas on this point see Chapter 9 of my earlier book, *The Role of Ethics in Social Theory*.

16. The philosophical critique of identity philosophy is associated with Theodor Adorno and with contemporary French poststructuralism. See the discussion in Peter Dews, "Adorno, Post-Structuralism and the Critique of Identity."

17. *Hegel's Logic*, p. 238.

II
The Dialectic of Alienation: Hegel's Theory of Greek Religion and Marx's Critique of Capital

1. See Marx's "Theses on Feuerbach," in Karl Marx and Frederick Engels *Collected Works*, volume 5, pp. 7-8; and his "Contribution to the Critique of Hegel's Philosophy of Law: Introduction," ibid., volume 3, pp. 175 ff. A classic study emphasizing the difference between Hegel and Marx's view of religion is Karl Löwith's *From Hegel to Nietzsche*, especially pp. 347 ff.

2. Hegel's presentation of Greek religion in the *Phenomenology* is quite different from that found in his later lectures on the philosophy of religion. Limitations of space, however, prevent me from exploring the differences in this chapter.

3. See the excellent study by Klaus Düsing, *Das Problem der Subjektivität in Hegels Logik*.

4. It is worth noting that, although epic poetry comes quite early in the history of Greek religion, from a systematic standpoint the epics express a complex form of religious consciousness. They thus come relatively late in Hegel's systematic ordering of religious forms in the *Phenomenology* (in his later lectures on religion, Hegel adheres closer to the historical order in his discussion of Greek religion).

5. All page numbers in the body of the text are to *The Phenomenology of Spirit*.

6. Hegel repeated this complaint on numerous occasions. In the course of his later lectures on Greek religion, he wrote: "The twelve principle gods of Olympus, for example, are not ordered by means of the concept. They do not constitute a system" (*Lectures on the Philosophy of Religion*, vol. 2, p. 654).

7. See Weber's "Religious Groups (The Sociology of Religion)," in his *Economy and Society*, vol. 2. passim.

8. "The hero is himself the speaker, and the performance displays to the audience — who are also spectators — *self-conscious* human beings who *know* their rights and purposes, the power and the will of their specific nature and know how to *assert* them" (*Phenomenology*, p. 444).

9. These characters *exist* as actual human beings who impersonate the heroes and portray them, not in the form of a narrative, but in the actual speech of the actors themselves" (*Ibid*).

10. The "crowd of spectators... have in the chorus their counterpart, or rather their own thought expressing itself" (p. 445)

11. The transition from religious concerns to sociopolitical matters may appear abrupt, but Hegel himself constantly combined the two. The precise relationship between religion and politics in Hegel's philosophy has been the matter of some dispute. Dilthey tended to see Hegel's politics as an expression of his religious convictions. In contrast, Lukacs tended to interpret Hegel's assertions regarding religion in terms of his political standpoint. (See Dilthey's *Die Jugendgeschichte Hegels*, vol. 4 of his *Gesammelte Schriften*; and *The Young Hegel* by Georg Lukacs.) Hegel's own view is probably captured more accurately by Walter Jaeschke. He writes, "The politicoeconomic and the theological perspectives are not isolated from each other; they are only different moments of one theory of *Sittlichkeit*" (*Die Relisionsphilosophie Hegels*, p. 37, my translation.) In this sense Hegel anticipated contemporary developments in liberation theology, where the polticoeconomic and the theological also are united.

12. Hegel's account of Greek tragedy generalizes his interpretation of Sophocles' *Antigone*.

13. "The doer finds himself thereby in the antithesis of knowing and not-knowing. He takes his purpose from this character and knows it as an ethical essentiality; but on account of the determinateness of his character he knows only the *one* power of substance, the other remaining for him concealed" (*Phenomenology*, p. 446).

14. The systematic reading of Marx's main works in economics is defended against the more orthodox historical reading in the following chapter.

15. Karl Marx, *Grundrisse*, p. 157.

16. Ibid., p. 146.

17. Karl Marx, *Theories of Surplus Value*, vol. 3, p. 272.

18. This is the topic of my *The Logic of Marx's "Capital."*

19. Hegel has been accused of a totalitarianism that does not leave any role for individuality. This critique has been made both by liberal critics (see Karl Popper's *The Open Society and it Enemies*, vol. 2) and by Marxist critics (see Lucio Colletti's *Marxism and Hegel*, discussed later in Chapter V). The section on comedy in the chapter on religion and the *Phenomenology* is just one of the many sections that reveals the extent to which this objection is based on utter ignorance of Hegel's position.

20. "The division of labour develops the *social* productive power of labour or the productive power of *social* labour, but at the expense of the *general productive ability* of the worker. This increase in *social productive power* confronts the worker therefore as an increased productive power, *not of his labour*, but of *capital*, the force that dominates his labour" (Marx, *Theories of Surplus Value*, vol. 2, p. 234).

21. Hegel's attempt to connect comedy with democracy does not seem entirely convincing. What are we to make of Aeschylus, a tragic poet who was a great proponent of democracy? (I owe this observation to my colleague, David Roochnik.)

22. Decades of Stalinism have covered over Marx's commitment to democracy. Marx insisted that under socialism all those holding public office would be elected and subject to recall. This was the policy of the Paris Commune, which Marx described as "the political form... under which to work out the economic emancipation of labour" ("The Civil War in France," Karl Marx and Frederick Engels, *Selected Writings*, p. 544; see also pp. 541-42).

23. The low level of technology attained in ancient Greece mandated that only a few had the leisure required to participate in the polis as full citizens. Marx felt that in a future society of advanced productive forces the material preconditions would be given for democratic practices far more advanced than those of ancient Greece.

24. "So opposed to the sovereignty of the monarch, the sovereignty of the people is one of the confused notions based on the wild idea of the 'people.' Taken without its monarch and the articulation of the whole which is the indispensable and direct concomitant of monarchy, the people is a formless mass and no longer a state" (G. W. F. Hegel, *Hegel's Philosophy of Right*, pp. 182-83). Klaus Hartman argued convincingly that Hegel's critique of democracy is inconsistent with his own philosophical principles in "Towards a New Systematic Reading of Hegel's *Philosophy of Right*."

25. See Ludger Oeing-Hanhoff's "Hegels Trinitätslehre. Zur Aufgabe ihrer Kritik und Rezeption"; Joerg Splett, *Die Trinitätslehre G. W. F. Hegel's*; and *Hegel's Trinitarian Claim*, by Dale M. Schlitt for accounts and evaluations of this dimension of Hegel's thought.

26. Michael Theunissen had concluded from this that the culmination of Hegel's philosophy or religion in Christianity counts as the culmination of his philosophy as a whole. (*Hegels Lehre vom absoluten Geist als theologischer-politischer Traktat*, pp. 254 ff). For a rejoinder see *Die Religionsphilosophie Hegels*, Jaeschke, p. 140.

27. In one sense the culminating form of Greek religion expresses this truth in a more adequate fashion than in Christianity. The latter always tends to revert to the picture thinking that places the divine somewhere beyond the community here and now: "Its own reconciliation therefore enters its consciousness as something in the distinct *past*" (478). This tendency is not present in Greek comedy. Of course, in Hegel's view this pales before the sense in which Christianity captures the truth of Spirit more deeply. For Christianity *all* individuals are in principle reconciled with the universal, whereas in ancient Greece women, slaves, wage laborers, and so forth were excluded from this reconciliation. It also should be noted in passing that in our interpretation of Hegel's philosophy of religion the traditional Marxist critique of that theory is thoroughly mistaken (see note 1). Hegel did not at all advocate an otherworldly diversion from the community that exists here and now. The culmination of his philosophy of religion is a turn to the community and not an escape from it.

28. With Christianity "the divine, the pure substance, had become human and internal to man, thus collapsing itself as a pure transcendent. . . . The abstractness of the separate, transcendent divine essence is collapsed and becomes but a moment of the action of living human beings. . . . Living in the Holy Spirit, I *am* divine; the divine is just the nature of the Holy Spirit in which I live, the concrete unity of the community of conscientious actors" (Joseph C. Flay, *Hegel's Quest for Certainty*, p. 237). See also "Endlichkeit und absoluter Geist in Hegels Philosophie" by Rolf Ahlers, pp. 63-80.

29. Such a critique is presented in detail by Richard Dien Winfield in his important book *The Just Economy*. For a reply see Chapter IV.

III
The Debate Regarding Dialectical Logic in Marx's Economic Writings

1. Other sorts of dialectical motifs can be found in Hegel, such as the "dialectics of nature." The controversy regarding this concept will not be examined here.

2. Marx and Engels, *Letters on "Capital"*, p. 50.

3. See Roman Rosdolsky, *The Making of Marx's "Capital."*

4. Hegel, *Hegel's Philosophy of Right*, p. 11.

5. For a fuller discussion of systematic dialectical theory, see Klaus Hartmann's "Hegel: A Non-Metaphysical View."

6. Karl Marx, *Grundrisse*, p. 100.

7. Ibid.

8. Ibid.

9. Ibid., p. 101.

10. *Hegel's Logic*, p. 177.

11. Marx, *Theories of Surplus Value*, vol. 2, p. 165.

12. Marx *Grundrisse*, p. 102. Compare this with the following passage from *Hegel's Philosophy of Right*: "What we acquire [in Hegel's systematic dialectic of categories] is a series of thoughts and another series of existent shapes of experience; to which I may add that the time order in which the latter actually appear is other than the logical order" (p. 233).

13. Marx, *Capital*, vol. 1, pp. 27-29.

14. Ibid., p. 29.

15. See Ronald Meek, *Economics and Ideology and Other Essays*, p. 96; and M. C. Howard and J. E. King, *The Political Economy of Marx*, pp. 46 ff. Of course, a great many other examples could be given as well. The logicohistorical reading of *Capital* is by far the most prevalent interpretation.

16. John Mepham, "From the *Grundrisse* to *Capital*: The Making of Marx's Method."

17. Gerhard Göhler, *Die Reduktion der Dialektik durch Marx*.

18. Hans-Georg Backhaus, "Materialien zur Rekonstrucktion der Marxschen Werttheorie."

19. See my *The Logic of Marx's "Capital."*

20. The development from barter, through exchange mediated by money, to exchange with money as an end has unmistakable historical overtones, to give just one example. In the work cited in the previous footnote, however, I show that Marx presented systematic arguments for these transitions as well.

21. E. von Böhm-Bawerk, *Karl Marx and the Close of his System*.

22. Karl Marx, *Theories of Surplus Value*, vol. 3, p. 163, emphasis added.

23. Briefly, Marx argued as follows. The *capital form* is defined as the social relation in which one class owns and controls the society's productive resources, thereby forcing another class to sell its labor power to it in order to survive. It is necessarily the case that the resulting wage contract will tend to reflect this asymmetry and allow the controllers of capital to appropriate an economic surplus produced by the wage laborers. In this sense there is a necessary connection between "the capital form" and "exploitation." See Chapter VII below.

24. See Chapter I on the importance of transitional goals for a dialectically informed politics.

25. Hegel's famous passage, "What is rational is actual and what is actual is rational" (*Hegel's Philosophy of Right*, p. 10) should not be read as a blanket endorsement of every aspect of the present social order. If that had been what he meant he would have used the category "existence" rather than that of "actuality," as examination of Hegel's *Logic* reveals. However in *The Philosophy of Right* Hegel does assert that the main structural features of the present order — generalized commodity exchange and the capitalist state — do not merely "exist," they are "actual" and therefore rational. They are to be affirmed. However, it also should be noted that in his youth Hegel held much more radical positions that anticipate Marx to an astonishing degree. See Jacques D'Hondt's *Hegel in His Time*.

IV
Hegel and Marx on Civil Society

1. A masterly presentation of this dimension of the Hegelian legacy in Marxism can be found in C. J. Arthur's *Dialectics of Labour: Marx and His Relation to Hegel*. On the role of means of production in Hegel, the following passage from *Hegel's Science of Logic* is most interesting: "In the means the rationality in it manifests itself as such by maintaining itself in *this external other*, and precisely *through* this externality. To this extent the *means* is *superior* to the *finite* ends of *external* purposiveness: the *plough* is more honourable than are immediately the enjoyments produced by it and which are ends. The *tool* lasts, while the immediate enjoyments pass away and are forgotten" (p. 747).

2. G. W. F. Hegel, *Hegel's Philosophy of Right*, pp. 148 ff.

3. David MacGregor, *The Communist Ideal in Hegel and Marx*, p. 259.

4. Ibid., p. 161.

5. *Philosophy of Right*, pp. 127 ff.

6. Ibid., p. 49.

7. Ibid., p. 148.

8. MacGregor, *The Communist Ideal*, p. 37.

9. Ibid., p. 244.

10. An exceptionally well-argued presentation of concrete instances of this dynamic can be found in Mike Davis's *Prisoners of the American Dream*.

11. MacGregor, *The Communist Ideal*, p. 141.

12. Hegel argued against the entire alienation of a person's powers through a contract (i.e., slavery) on the grounds that this involves the complete subordination of the will of one person by another. But he did allow a piecemeal alienation of a worker's time that has the same result, the appropriation of one person's

entire labor time by another. As Arthur points out in the book cited in note 1, this is incoherent.

13. Richard Dien Winfield, *The Just Economy*, p. 61.

14. Ibid., p. 67.

15. Karl Marx, *Grundrisse*, p. 409.

16. Karl Marx, *Capital*, vol. 1, p. 48. It must be granted that some Marxists have defended a purely technical interpretation of the notion of socially necessary labor. The definitive refutation of this interpretation is found in I. I. Rubin's *Essays on Marx's Theory of Value*.

17. Winfield, *The Just Economy*, p. 110.

18. Ibid., p. 161.

19. Ibid., p. 143

20. Ibid., p. 139

21. Ibid., p. 111.

22. Given the absence of an explicitly formulated law and impartial judges to apply and enforce that law, it is necessarily the case that even well-intentioned individuals often will dispute which of them has the rightful property in a thing ("nonmalicious wrong"). Given this state of affairs, it is necessarily the case that some social agents often will feign a right to a thing that they know they do not have ("fraud"). Finally, the absence of enforcement mechanisms regulating property rights also necessarily generates a tendency for some to seize the property of others ("crime"). See *Hegel's Philosophy of Right*. pp. 64-73.

23. Ibid., p. 129.

24. A defense of Marx's theory is found in my *The Logic of Marx's Capital*.

25. Winfield, *The Just Economy*, p. 114.

26. Ibid., p. 121.

27. Ibid., p. 125.

28. Ibid., pp. 95-96.

29. Ibid., p. 98.

30. Ibid., p. 129.

31. Of course, in many cases the procedures of democratic planning would *not* be agreed to by social agents. These concern decisions inherently private in nature, such as the choice of a companion. Control of society's productive resources, however, is not an inherently private matter (at least not once the process of concentration and centralization has proceeded past a certain point). It involves the exercise of public power, one that may affect the public more than most decisions made by state officials. It therefore is fully appropriate to subject this exercise of public power to public control.

32. The production period would begin only after an extensive period of public discussion. As I stressed in Chapter I, socialist democracy involves more than voting. See Part Three of my earlier work, *The Role of Ethics in Social Theory*, for an elaboration of socialist democracy and a comparison between it and the normative models of institutions defended by Kant, Rawls, and Habermas.

V
Hegelianism and Marx: A Reply to Lucio Colletti

1. Frederick Engels, *Socialism: Utopian and Scientific* pp. 8-9.

2. All citations without further reference are to this work.

3. This is especially the case in Great Britain. For example, Perry Anderson, the editor of the influential *New Left Review*, has written, "Lucio Colletti once remarked: 'One could say that there are two main traditions in Western philosophy in this respect: one that descends from Spinoza and Hegel, and the other from Hume and Kant. For any theory that takes science as the sole form of real knowledge [such as Marxism] there can be no question that the tradition of Hume-Kant must be given priority and preference over that of Spinoza-Hegel.' The broad truth of this claim is incontrovertible." *Arguments Within English Marxism*, p. 6. The passage Anderson quotes is found in "A Political and Philosophical Interview," p. 11.

4. Pp. 115-16.

5. P. 116.

6. P. 116.

7. P. 16.

8. P. 17.

9. P. 121.

10. P. 7.

11. P. 8.

12. P. 69.

13. "The act by which *he* abstracts from or discounts the finite can now be represented by Hegel as an *objective* movement carried out by the finite itself in order to go beyond itself and thus *pass over* into its essence" (15).

14. P. 12. Colletti described this process as a "tautoheterology"; the finite appears to be distinct from (heterogeneous to) the infinite, but the actual situation is a "tautology" in which the finite *is* nothing but the incarnation of the infinite.

15. Colletti believed that, in Hegel, "The world was negated in order to give way to the immanentization of God; the finite was 'idealized' so that the

Christian *Logos* could incarnate itself and so that the infinite could pass over from the beyond into the here and now" (80).

16. Colletti devoted an entire chapter (Chapter 11) to the identity of the philosophies of Spinoza and Hegel.

17. This was Marx's point when he wrote that in Hegel's thought "the empirical fact has in its empirical existence another significance other than itself. The fact which is one's point of departure is not apprehended as such, but only as mystical effect," quoted in Colletti, p. 20.

18. P. 198.

19. "The breaking of the 'mystical shell' and thus the 'overturning' of the dialectic...can only consist in the recovery of the principle of identity and non-contradiction or, what is the same thing, the recovery of the materialist point of view" (48).

20. "Hegel is the first to understand thoroughly how man's development passes through his self-objectification and how this process of making himself 'other' than himself is carried out, essentially, by means of work" (222).

21. "From Kant...Marx clearly derives — whether he was aware of it or not, and whatever may have been the process of mediation — the principle of real existence as something 'more' with respect to everything contained in the concept" (122).

22. "Whereas 'dialectical materialism', in order to be materialist, needed precisely that 'something more', it has instead adopted Hegel's 'dialectic of matter', i.e., the proposition that all things 'are' and 'are not', without realizing that the basis of that dialectic was precisely the *negation* or the 'destruction' of that 'something more'" (103).

23. "Horkheimer and Adorno represent a limiting case. Together with Marcuse, they are the most conspicuous example of the extreme confusion that can be reached by mistaking the romantic critique of intellect and science for a socio-historical critique of capitalism" (175).

24. Pp. 194-95.

25. See Chapter III, as well as my study *The Logic of Marx's Capital*. A number of other comparisons of the philosophical frameworks employed by Hegel and Marx should be mentioned: H. G. Backhaus, "Zur Dialectik der Wertform"; H. J. Krahl, "Zum Verhaltnis von 'Kapital' und Hegelscher Wesenslogik"; Hans Reichelt, *Zur logischen Struktur des Kapitalbegriffs*; Roman Rosdolsky, *The Making of Marx's "Capital"*; and Klaus Hartmann, *Die Marxsche Theorie*.

26. Karl Marx, *Grundrisse*, p. 100.

27. *Hegel's Philosophy of Right*, p. 11.

28. Marx, *Grundrisse*, p. 100.

29. G. W. F. Hegel, *Lectures on the History of Philosophy*, vol. 3, pp. 175-76. Consider also these statements from Hegel's *Logic* (Part One of his *Encyclopaedia*): "The point of departure [for philosophy] is Experience; including under that name both our immediate consciousness and the inductions from it.... The sciences, based on experience, exert upon the mind a stimulus.... In consequence of this stimulus thought [i.e., philosophy] is dragged out of its unrealized universality and its fancied or merely possible satisfaction, and impelled onwards to a development from itself... thought incorporates the contents of science, in all their speciality of detail as submitted.... Experience is the real author of *growth* and *advance* in philosophy.... The reception into philosophy of these scientific materials, now that thought has removed their immediacy and made them cease to be mere data, forms at the same time a development of thought out of itself. Philosophy, then owes its development to the empirical sciences" (Section 12, pp. 16 ff).

30. See Hegel's "With What Must the Science Begin?" in *Hegel's Science of Logic*, pp. 79 ff.

31. Marx, *Grundrisse*, p. 100.

32. Ibid., p. 101.

33. *Hegel's Philosophy of Right*, p. 233.

34. See Jindřich Zelený, *Die Wissenschaftslogik bei Marx und "Das Kapital."*

35. Marx, p. 107.

36. Ernest Mandel, in *Marxist Economic Theory*, reads Marx in this manner.

37. Marx, *Grundrisse*, p. 101.

38. Hegel, *History of Philosophy*, vol. 3, pp. 176-77.

39. In his *Philosophy of History* Hegel speculated that the future course of world history may revolve around the Americas. But this is not presented as something deduced with necessity and he immediately adds that "as a Land of the Future. it [the New World] has no interest for us here" (p. 87).

40. "Individual souls are distinguished from one another by an infinite number of contingent modifications" (*The Philosophy of Mind*, p. 51).

41. "In the particularization of the content in sensation, the *contingency* and one-sided subjective form of that content is established" (ibid., pp. 74-75).

42. The market "subjects the permanent existence of even the entire family to dependence on itself and to contingency.... Not only caprice, however, but also contingencies, physical conditions, and factors grounded in external circumstances may reduce men to poverty" (*Hegel's Philosophy of Right*, p. 148).

43. In positive law "there may enter the contingency of self-will and other particular circumstances" (ibid., p. 136).

44. Logically, an abstract unity that does not include differences within it precedes the fragmentation of that abstract unity into an aggregate of different entities, which in turn precedes the reestablishment of a unity on a higher level, a concrete unity that includes differences within it. And so Hegel was able to pick out a thread of intelligibility in world history in which a logical order progresses from the Greek polis (abstract unity), through Rome and Roman Law (difference, fragmentation), to the modern state (concrete unity-in-difference). But Hegel by no means included all historical events within the logical ordering of historical stages that constitutes his philosophy of history. Events occurring elsewhere than at the particular place where the specific stage of universal history is unfolding are not included in the logical ordering. On the place of "contingency" in Hegel's system in general, see Dieter Henrich's "Hegels Theorie uber den Zufall."

45. This is the well-known double meaning of Hegel's term *Aufhebung*, "sublation." It connotes overcoming and preservation at once.

46. The faculty Colletti referred to as "intellect" usually is rendered as "understanding" by Hegel's English translators. Regarding this faculty Hegel wrote that, "The merit and rights of the mere Understanding should unhesitatingly be admitted. And that merit lies in the fact that apart from Understanding there is no fixity or accuracy in the region of theory or of practice" (*Logic* [Encyclopaedia], #80, pp. 113-14).

47. "This school makes sense-perception the form in which fact is to be apprehended; and in this consists the defect of Empiricism. Sense-perception as such is always individual, always transient; not indeed that the process of knowledge stops short at sensation: on the contrary, it proceeds to find out the universal and permanent element in the individual apprehended by sense. This is the process leading from simple perception to experience" (ibid., #38, p. 62). For our purposes *empiricism* may be taken as equivalent to *nominalism* here.

48. This totality Hegel termed *the Idea*: "The unity of determinate existence [i.e., individual things] and the concept [i.e., the universal]...is the Idea." (*Hegel's Philosophy of Right*, p. 225).

49. G. W. F. Hegel, *Natural Law*, pp. 92 ff.

50. *Hegel's Philosophy of Right*. p. 254.

51. Ibid., pp. 155-56 (emphasis added).

52. "The universal does not prevail or achieve completion except along with particular interests and through the co-operation of particular knowing and willing.... The principle of modern states had prodigious strength and depth because it allows the principle of subjectivity to progress to its culmination in the extreme of self-subsistent personal particularity, and yet at the same time brings it back to the substantive unity and so maintains this unity in the principle of subjectivity itself" (*Hegel's Philosophy of Right*, #260, pp. 160-61). "In whatever

way an individual may fulfill his duty, he must at the same time find his account therein and attain his personal interest and satisfaction. Out of his position in the state, a right must accrue to him whereby public affairs shall be his own particular affair. Particular interests should in fact not be set aside or completely suppressed; instead they should be put in correspondence with the universal, and thereby both they and the universal are upheld" (ibid., #261, p. 162).

53. I would like to stress that I am defending the general ontological framework underlying Hegel's theory of the state, not the specifics of that theory itself.

54. P. 46.

55. P. 18.

56. "Substantive freedom is the abstract undeveloped Reason implicit in volition, proceeding to develop itself in the State. But in this [premodern] phase of Reason there is still wanting personal insight and will, that is, subjective freedom; which is realized only in the Individual, and which constitutes the reflection of the Individual in his own conscience" (*Philosophy of History*, p. 104). It is because the principle of subjective freedom is recognized in the modern period that Hegel saw it as an advance over the premodern era.

57. Colletti devoted an entire chapter to a conflation of Spinoza and Hegel. It is remarkable that he nowhere discussed Hegel's own evaluation of Spinoza in his *Lectures on the History of Philosophy*, vol. 3. Hegel could not be more explicit there. Although Spinoza is an ally in the struggle against those content with a one-tiered ontology, Spinoza's negation of the individual shows that he did not attain the level of the *Begriff*: "When Spinoza passes on to individual things, especially to self-consciousness, to the freedom of the 'I', he expresses himself in such a way as rather to lead back all limitations to substance than to maintain a firm grasp of the individual" (ibid., p. 269). "There is, in his system, an utter blotting out of the principle of subjectivity, individuality, personality" (ibid., p. 287). It is true that in youthful writings such as the *Jenaer Logik* Hegel's position was quite close to Spinoza. But the development of his thought can be traced precisely in terms of his overcoming the Spinozaism of his early works. This has been established in detail by Klaus Düsing in his *Das Problem der Subjektivität in Hegels Logik*.

58. Colletti does not merely fail to quote relevant passages from Hegel. He also failed to note Marx's own acknowledgment of Hegel's influence; for instance, the passage already cited in the second note of Chapter III.

59. Karl Marx, *Theories of Surplus Value*, vol. 2, p. 509.

60. Ibid., p. 500.

61. "[The Commune's] true secret was this. It was essentially a working-class government, the product of the struggle of the producing against the appropri-

ating class, the political form at last discovered under which to work out the economic emancipation of labour" ("The Civil War in France," Marx, *Selections*, p. 544). The three features mentioned in the main text are discussed on pp. 541-42. See the discussion of this normative model of institutions in my *The Role of Ethics in Social Theory*, passim.

62. Marx and Engels, "The German Ideology," in *Collected Works*, vol. 5, p. 78.

63. Theses on Feuerbach," in ibid., p. 6. See also Mandel, *Late Capitalism*, p. 17.

64. Hegel, *Philosophy of History*, p. 18.

65. Ibid., p. 416.

66. Marx and Engels, "The German Ideology," in *Collected Works*, vol. 5, p. 53.

67. On property rights cf. *Hegel's Philosphy of Right*, Part One ("Abstract Right"), on children's rights, #174, on freedom of speech, #319, and on various civil rights see the entire section entitled "The Administration of Justice." Recent scholarship on Hegel's political writings has emphasized these liberal elements in Hegel's thought and thoroughly refuted the view of Hegel as precusor of totalitarianism. See the collection of essays in Z. A. Pelczynski, ed., *Hegel's Political Philosophy: Problems and Perspectives*.

VI
Elster's Critique of Marx's Systematic Dialectical Theory

1. See Karl Popper's "What Is Dialectics?" for a classic statement of the traditional hostility of analytical philosophers towards dialectics.

2. *Analytical Marxism* is a catch-all term that has been used to group together a number of diverse perspectives (Buchanan, "Marx, Morality, and History"). In this and the next chapter I restrict the term to the "rational choice Marxism" of John Elster and John Roemer.

3. John Roemer, "'Rational Choice' Marxism: Some Issues of Method and Substance," p. 191.

4. John Elster, *Making Sense of Marx*, pp. 41-2.

5. Ibid., p. 44.

6. Ibid., p. 37.

7. Ibid., p. 37. It at least should be mentioned that most dialecticians would be no more willing to accept this division of theoretical labor than Elster. They would insist that dialectical thinking has a much greater role to play in the social science than that granted by Elster. See Joseph McCarney's important review of Elster, "A New Marxist Paradigm?"

8. Elster, *Making Sense of Marx*, p. 40.

9. Ibid., p. 37.

10. Ibid., p. 38.

11. Ibid., p. 39.

12. Ibid., p. 38.

13. Ibid., p. 38.

14. Karl Marx, *Grundrisse*, p. 270. See also Terrance Carver's "Marx – and Hegel's Logic."

15. Elster, *Making Sense of Marx*, p. 39.

16. Ibid., p. 39. See the appendix to Chapter 7 in Roemer's *A General Theory of Exploitation and Class*.

17. Hegel, *Lectures on the Philosophy of Religion*, vol. 3, p. 271.

18. The most important rule already was introduced in Chapter I. Categories of simple unity lead to categories of difference, which in turn lead to categories of unity-in-difference. A category is a principle that unifies a manifold. From this it follows that there are three fundamental sorts of categorial structures. One emphasizes the moment of unity. One emphasizes the moment of difference, the manifold. And one expresses a more or less precarious balance of these two moments within a structure of unity-in-difference. Dialectical progressions of categories that are systematically arranged from the simplest and most abstract to the more complex and concrete move from categories of simple unity to categories of difference, and then to categories of unity-in-difference, which then form categories of simple unity at a higher categorical level. These and other complications of dialectical logic, however, are not relevant in the present context and will not be pursued further.

19. Marx, *Grundrisse*, p. 107.

20. Elster, *Making Sense of Marx*, p. 122.

21. Not all analytical Marxists have failed to see this: two examples are Alan Wood (*Karl Marx*, pp. 197, 216-34) and Kai Nielsen (*Marxism and the Moral Point of View*, p. 288).

22. For example, it has been shown that Hegel's derivation of the monarchy in *The Philosophy of Right* was an *ad hoc* transition that violated Hegel's own methodological cannons. See Klaus Hartmann's "Towards a New Systematic Reading of Hegel's *Philosophy of Right*."

23. Although the search for microfoundations is compatible with dialectical Marxism, the methodological individualism characteristic of rational choice Marxism is not. For a compelling critique of the methodological individualism defended by Elster, see Levine, Sober, and Wright, "Marxism and Methodological Individualism." These authors also pointed out that rational choice explanations do not provide the only sort of microfoundational account:

"There are many other possible kinds of microfoundations of social phenomena. Theories of socialization which emphasize the inculcation of norms, habits and rituals, or even psychoanalytic theories of the unconscious can be used. The Marxist theory of ideology, understood as a theory of the process of forming social subjects, can also provide a basis for elaborating microfoundations" (p. 83).

24. *Hegel's Philosophy of Right*. pp. 57 ff.

25. Marx. *Grundrisse*, p. 107.

26. The reader who seeks a fuller account of Marx's systematic ordering of categories than can be provided here may consult Rosdolsky's *The Making of Marx's "Capital"* and my *The Logic of Marx's "Capital."*

27. Elster, *Making Sense of Marx*, p. 310.

28. Marx, *Capital*, vol. 1, p. 43.

29. Marx, *Grundrisse*, p. 776.

30. Elster, *Making Sense of Marx*, p. 312.

31. Ibid., p. 140.

32. Ibid., p. 127-38. Elster here repeated Ian Steedman's *Marx After Sraffa*.

33. Marx, *Capital*, vol. 3, pp. 819-20.

34. "Nothing can have value, without being an object of utility" (*Capital*, vol. 1, p. 41). Commodities "must show that they are use-values before they can be realised as values. For the labour spent upon them counts effectively, only in so far as it is spent in a form that is useful for others" (ibid., p. 89). Michio Morishima draws the proper conclusion from such passages: "On the basis of the evidence I believe that Marx would have accepted the marginal utility theory of consumer's demands if it had become known to him" (*Marx's Economics*, p. 40).

35. Anwar Shaikh, "The Transformation from Marx to Sraffa."

36. This point is made by I. I. Rubin in *Essays on Marx's Theory of Value*, and by Chris Arthur in his article "Dialectic of the Value-Form."

37. "The seller turned his commodity into money, in order thereby to satisfy some want; the hoarder did the same in order to keep his commodity in its money-shape, and the debtor in order to be able to pay.... The value-form of commodities, money, is therefore now the end and aim of a sale, and that owing to a social necessity springing out of the process of circulation itself" (*Capital*, vol. 1, p. 136). This spells out the microfoundation for the transition from $C \rightarrow M \rightarrow C$ to the $M \rightarrow C \rightarrow M$ circuit. The microfoundation for the transition to capital, to the $M \rightarrow C \rightarrow M^1$ circuit, follows at once: "Now it is evident that the circuit $M - C - M$ would be absurd and without meaning if the intention were to exchange by this means two equal sums of money" (ibid., p. 146).

38. Elster, *Making Sense of Marx*, p. 255.

39. Marx, *Selections*, pp. 187-91.

40. Elster did briefly consider a definition of exploitation that included the notion of control of the produced surplus. However he dismissed it at once with the comment that this usage was "distinctly unusual" (*Making Sense of Marx*, p. 177). This is mistaken; it is not at all unusual in Marx. In all of Marx's writings there is no single place where exploitation terms are used and the exploited agents have control over the allocation of the produced surplus.

41. Max Weber, *Economy and Society*, vol. 1. It should be noted that the systematic section of *Economy and Society* orders categories that supposedly apply to all social formations, whereas Marx's systematic works are limited to the reconstruction of a historically specific mode of production. This does not affect the point being made.

VII
Roemer on Marx's Theory of Exploitation: Shortcomings of a Non-Dialectical Approach

1. John Roemer, "Property Relations vs. Surplus Value in Marxian Exploitation," pp. 282-83.

2. Ibid.

3. Roemer, "Exploitation, Class, and Property Relations," pp. 197-99.

4. Roemer, "Unequal Exchange, Labor Migration and International Capital Flows."

5. Roemer, "Should Marxists Be Interested in Exploitation?" pp. 274-75.

6. Ibid., pp. 275-76.

7. For example, Michael Lebowitz has pointed out the difficulties Roemer falls into as a result of ignoring the distinction between labor and labor power ("Is Analytical Marxism Marxism?"). Anderson and Thompson rejected Roemer's analysis on the grounds that it cannot account for the class consciousness that may emerge in response to exploitation ("Neoclassical Marxism").

8. Karl Marx, *Grundrisse*, p. 101.

9. This is taken up in length in my *The Logic of Marx's "Capital."*

10. Marx, *Capital*, vol. 1, p. 166.

11. Roemer, "Property Relations vs. Surplus Value," p. 289.

12. Marx, *Capital*, vol. 1, p. 322. That Marx defended the existence of "fundamental principles of the human condition" has been conclusively established by Norman Geras in *Marx and Human Nature: Refutation of a Legend*.

13. Roemer, "Exploitation, Class, and Property Relations," p. 209.

14. Marx and Engels, *Selected Writings*, pp. 564 ff.

15. Roemer himself recently came to note this. See "Should Marxists Be Interested in Exploitation?" p. 270.

16. Marx, *Capital*, vol. 3, p. 609.

17. Marx wrote that "In countries . . . where the capitalist mode of production is already in existence but which have to compete with far more developed countries [i.e., countries with more capital intensive production], labour-time is excessively long" (*Theories of Surplus Value*, vol. 2, p. 16).

18. For a discussion of the various formulations of Marx's complete system see Rosdolsky's *The Making of Marx's "Capital,"* Chapter 2.

19. V. I. Lenin, "Conspectus of Hegel's Book *The Science of Logic*," p. 180.

VIII
The Critique of Marxism in Baudrillard's Late Writings

1. Arthur Kroker in his book *The Postmodern Scene* has proposed that Baudrillard should be seen as a Marxist albeit one who has grasped the necessity of reading Marx in terms of Nietzsche. In Kroker's reading of *Capital* the principle underlying the circuit of capital is the will to will of which Nietzsche spoke. This is an interesting suggestion, but it cannot be accepted. For one thing, for every fundamental Marxist thesis that Baudrillard turned out to share there are a multitude that he rejected. For another, Baudrillard himself has explicitly rejected this sort of suggestion. When asked if he is a person of the Left or Right he answered "I can no longer function according to this criterion" ("Intellectual Commitment and Political Power: An Interview with Jean Baudrillard," p. 171). Most important, there is the substantive dimension of Kroker's case. Kroker interpreted the Marxist category of capital in terms of Nietzsche's will to will. But Marx's concern was with specific sorts of will: the will to accumulate (forced on capitalists by the logic of market competition), the will to resist capital accumulation (forced on wage laborers by that same logic), and so on. The "will to will" is abstract, and it covers over class distinctions. Concepts of will with these two features were consistently rejected by Marx.

2. Baudrillard, *The Mirror of Production*.

3. The best account of the Marxist notion of ideology is found in Joseph McCarney's *The Real World of Ideology*.

4. "The Precession of Simulacra," in *Simulations*, p. 4.

5. "Forget Baudrillard," in *Forget Foucault*, p. 90.

6. ". . . Or the End of the Social," in *In the Shadow of the Silent Majorities . . . Or the End of the Social; and Other Essays*, p. 89.

7. "In the Shadow of the Silent Majorities," ibid., p. 56.

8. "...Or the End of the Social," p. 84.

9. "Forget Foucault," in *Forget Foucault*, p. 27.

10. "...Or the End of the Social," p. 89.

11. "The Orders of Simulacra," in *Simulations*, pp. 147-48. Also see the passage quoted in note 27.

12. "In the Shadow of the Silent Majorities," p. 27. "All the movements which only bet on liberation, emancipation, the resurrection of the subject of history, of the group, of speech as a raising of consciousness, indeed of a 'seizure of the inconscious' of subjects and of the masses, do not see that they are acting in accordance with the system, whose imperative today is the overproduction and regeneration of meaning and speech" ("The Implosion of Meaning in the Media," in *In the Shadow*, p. 109).

13. "The Procession of Simulacra," p. 4. The rejection of the specific referent *needs* goes back to Baudrillard's earliest writings, collected in *For a Critique of the Political Economy of the Sign*, especially "The Ideological Genesis of Needs" and "Beyond Use Value." See also *The Mirror of Production*, pp. 28, 32, and passim.

14. Ibid., p. 25.

15. Ibid., p. 48.

16. "The Implosion of Meaning in the Media," in *In the Shadow*, p. 108. There is no positive act here; instead an "absence of response" is lauded as a counterstrategy of the masses in the age of simulation (ibid., p. 105).

17. "Forget Foucault," p. 56.

18. '...Or the End of the Social," p. 70. See also *The Mirror of Production*, p. 158.

19. "Forget Foucault," p. 58.

20. '...Or the End of the Social," p. 85.

21. Ibid., p. 86.

22. "Forget Baudrillard," pp. 127-29.

23. "In the Shadow of the Silent Majorities," p. 56.

24. "Forget Baudrillard," p. 90.

25. "Forget Foucault," p. 25-26.

26. "The Precession of Simulacra," p. 31.

27. In our world "art and industry exchange their signs... Production can lose all social finality so as to be verified and exalted finally in the prestigious, hyperbolic signs that are the great industrial combines, the ¼ mile high towers or the number mysticism of the GNP... art is everywhere, since artifice is the very heart of reality" ("The Orders of Simulacra," p. 151). Mark Poster's "Semiology and

Critical Theory: from Marx to Baudrillard" provides a good overview of this aspect of Baudrillard's thought. Its importance for an understanding of contemporary culture has been explored by Victor Burgin in *The End of Art Theory: Criticism and Postmodernity*.

28. I would like to note in passing that developments in information technology that confirm the Marxist position undermine a number of other currents that proclaim themselves post-Marxist. Lyotard, who also claims to be beyond Marx, called for the means of producing information to be made available to all. In this era of ever increasing concentration and centralization of information technology in the hands of capital, the naivete of this position is staggering. See his *The Postmodern Condition: A Report on Knowledge*, p. 67.

29. "The Precession of Simulacra," p. 28. "The liberating practices respond to *one* of the aspects of the system, to the constant ultimatum to make of ourselves pure objects, but they don't respond at all to the other demand, which is to constitute ourselves as subjects, to liberate ourselves, to express ourselves at any price" ("The Implosion of Meaning in the Media," p. 108).

30. In Chapter IV we saw that Winfield made this same mistake. In the present context we should again recall that Marx pointed to "The discovery, creation and satisfaction of new needs arising from society itself; the cultivation of all the qualities of the social human being, production of the same in a form as rich as possible in needs, because rich in qualities and relations – production of this being as the most total and universal possible social product, for, in order to take gratification in a many-sided way, he must be capable of many pleasures, hence cultured to a high degree – is likewise a condition of production founded on capital.... The development of a constantly expanding and more comprehensive system of different kinds of labour, different kinds of production, to which a constantly expanding and constantly enriched system of needs corresponds" (*Grundrisse*, p. 409). This is very far from the crassly naturalistic theory of needs Baudrillard imputed to Marx.

31. For critical discussions of Baudrillard's rejection of the category of needs, see Robert Hefner's article "Baudrillard's Noble Anthropology: The Image of Symbolic Exchange in Political Economy," and "Postmodernism in a French Context" by Patrick Murray and Jeanne Schuler. A clear exposition and defense of Baudrillard's position is found in "Sociology in the Absence of the Social: The Significance of Baudrillard for Contemporary Thought" by William Bogard.

32. I discuss Habermas's theory of truth at length in Chapters I and X of my *The Role of Ethics in Social Theory: Essays from a Habermasian Perspective*.

33. See "The Precession of Simulacra," pp. 26-27.

34. Ibid., p. 34.

35. This element of repetition is a crucial component of Baudrillard's definition of simulacra, which are "produced from miniaturised units, from matrices,

memory banks and command models — and with these it can be reproduced an indefinite number of times" (ibid., p. 3). "For the sign to be pure it has to duplicate itself: it is the duplication of the sign which destroys its meaning" ("The Orders of Simulacra," p. 136). The paradigm is the genetic code, meaninglessly producing endless derivations of itself without any sort of finality (ibid., p. 105).

36. Ibid., p. 125.

37. Ibid., p. 133.

38. "The Precession of Simulacra," p. 12.

39. Angela Davis, *Women, Race and Class*, Chapter 11.

40. Never one to be overly concerned with elementary consistency, Baudrillard recently said that "I hold no position on reality. Reality remains an unsinkable postulate." Now he insists that his point is that reality is like seismatic shifts of plates of the earth: "The seismatic is our form of the slipping and sliding of the referential.... Nothing remains but shifting movements that provoke very powerful raw events.... Things no longer meet head-on; they slip past one another" ("Forget Baudrillard," pp. 125-26). With this return of the repressed referent, however, any attempt to justify a rejection of Marxism on the grounds that it holds to a reality principle dissolves. For Marx's project was precisely to understand these shifting movements.

41. "Forget Foucault," p. 44. We have seen that elsewhere Baudrillard wrote that "dialectical polarity no longer exists." But does not the fact that the position of exploiter and exploited cannot be reversed suggest that indeed there is a "dialectical polarity" in this relation?

42. Ibid., p. 112.

43. Ibid., p. 48.

Selected Bibliography

Ahlers, Rolf. "Endlichkeit und absoluter Geist in Hegels Philosophie." *Zeitschrift fur philosophische Forschung* 29 (1975).

Albert, Michael, and R. Hahnel. *Socialism Today and Tomorrow*. Boston: South End Press, 1981.

Anderson, W. H. Locke, and Frank W. Thompson. "Neoclassical Marxism." *Science and Society* 52, no. 2 (1988).

Anderson. Perry. *Arguments Within Western Marxism*. London: Verso, 1980.

Arthur, Chris J. "Dialectic of the Value-Form." In Elson. 1979.

______. *Dialectics of Labour: Marx and His Relation to Hegel*. New York: Basil Blackwell, 1984.

Backhaus, H. G. "Zur Dialektik der Wertform." In Schmidt, 1969.

______. "Materialien zur Rekonstruktion der Marxschen Werttheorie." *Gesellschaft: Beiträge zur Marxschen Theorie*, nos. 1 (1974), 3 (1975), 11 (1978).

Balbus, Isacc D. *Marxism and Domination: A Neo-Hegelian, Feminist, Psychoanalytic Theory of Sexual, Political, and Technological Liberation*. Princeton, N.J.: Princeton University Press, 1982.

Ball, Terence, and J. Farr. *After Marx*. Cambridge: Cambridge University Press, 1984.

Baudrillard, Jean. *The Mirror of Production*. St. Louis: Telos Press, 1975.

______. *For a Critique of the Political Economy of the Sign*. St. Louis: Telos Press, 1981.

______. *Simulations*. New York: Semiotext(e), 1983.

______. *In the Shadow of the Silent Majorities... Or the End of the Social; and Other Essays*. New York: Semiotext(e), 1983.

______. "Intellectual Commitment and Political Power: An Interview with Jean Baudrillard." *Thesis Eleven*, nos. 10-11 (1984-85).

______. *Forget Foucault*. New York: Semiotext(e), 1987.

Benton, Ted. *The Rise and Fall of Structural Marxism: Althusser and His Influence*. London: Macmillan, 1984.

Bogard, William. "Sociology in the Absence of the Social: The Significance of Baudrillard for Contemporary Thought." *Philosophy and Social Criticism* 13 (1987).

Böhm-Bawerk, Eugen von. *Karl Marx and the Close of His System*. New York: Augustus M. Kelly, 1949.

Buchanan, Alan. "Marx, Morality, and History: An Assessment of Recent Analytical Work on Marx." *Ethics* 98 (1987).

Burgin, Victor. *The End of Art Theory: Criticism and Postmodernity*. London: Macmillan, (1986).

Carver, Terrance. "Marx — and Hegel's *Logic*." *Political Studies* 24, (1976).

Colletti, Lucio. "A Political and Philosophical Interview. *New Left Review* 86, (1974).

______. *Marxism and Hegel*. London: Verso Press, 1979.

Davis, Angela. *Women, Race and Class*. New York: Vintage Press, 1983.

Davis, Mike. *Prisoners of the American Dream*. London: Verso Press, 1986.

Desai, Padma, ed. *Marxism, the Soviet Economy and Central Planning*. Cambridge, Mass.: MIT Press, 1983.

Dews, Peter. "Adorno, Post-Structuralism and the Critique of Identity." *New Left Review* 157, (1986).

D'Hondt, Jacques. *Hegel in His Time: Berlin 1818-1831*. Lewiston, N.Y.: Broadview Press, 1988.

Dilthey, Wilhelm. *Die Jugendgeschichte Hegels*. Gesammelte Schriften vol. 4. Stuttgart: B. G. Teuchner, 1959.

Düsing, Klaus. *Das Problem der Sujecktivitält in Hegels Logik*. Bonn: Hegel Studien Beiheft 15, 1976.

Elson, Diane, ed. *Value: The Representation of Labour in Capitalism*. Atlantic Highlands, N.J.: Humanities Press, 1979.

Elster, Jon. *Making Sense of Marx*. Cambridge: Cambridge University Press, 1985.

Engels, Fredrick. *Socialism: Utopian and Scientific*. Peking: Foreign Languages Press, 1975.

Flay, Joseph C. *Hegel's Quest for Certainty*. Albany: SUNY Press, 1984.

Geras, Norman. *Marx and Human Nature: Refutation of a Legend*. London: New Left Books, 1983.

Göhler, Gerhard. *Die Reduktion der Dialektik durch Marx*. Stuttgart: Klett-Cotta, 1980.

Gottlieb, Roger. *History and Subjectivity: The Transformation of Marxist Theory*. Philadelphia: Temple University Press, 1987.

Habermas, Jürgen. *Theorie des kommunikativen Handelns* 2 volumes. Frankfurt: Suhrkamp, 1981.

Hartmann, Klaus. *Die Marxsche Theorie*. Berlin: De Gruyter, 1970.

______. "Hegel: A Non-Metaphysical View." In MacIntyre, 1972.

______. ed. *Die Ontologishe Option*. Berlin: Walter De Gruyter, 1976.

______. "Towards a New Systematic Reading of Hegel's *Philosophy of Right*." In Pelczynski, 1984.

Hefner, Robert. "Baudrillard's Noble Anthropology: The Image of Symbolic Exchange in Political Economy." *Sub-stance*, no. 17, (1977).

Hegel, G. W. F. *Hegel's Philosophy of Right*,. New York: Oxford University Press, 1942.

______. *Lectures on the History of Philosophy*, 3 volumes. London: Routledge & Kegan Paul, 1955.

______. *The Philosophy of History*, New York: Dover Books, 1956.

______. *Hegel's Science of Logic*. London: Allen and Unwin, 1969.

______. *The Philosophy of Mind*. New York: Oxford University Press, 1971.

______. *Natural Law*. Philadelphia: University of Pennsylvania Press, 1971.

______. *Lectures on the Philosophy of Religion*, 3 volumes. New York: Humanities Press, 1974.

______. *Hegel's Logic*. (Encyclopedia version). New York: Oxford University Press, 1975.

______. *Phenomenology of Spirit*. Oxford: Oxford University Press, 1977.

______. *Lectures on the Philosophy of Religion*, vol. 2, Berkeley: University of California Press, 1987.

Henrich, Dieter. "Hegels Theorie uber den Zufall." In *Hegel in Kontext*. Frankfurt: Suhrkamp, 1971.

Howard, M. C., and J. E. King. *The Political Economy of Marx*. London: Longman, 1975.

Inwood, M. J., ed. *Hegel*. New York: Oxford University Press, 1985.

Jaeschke, Walter. *Die Religionsphilosophie Hegels*. Darmstadt: Wissenschaftliche Buchgesellschaft, 1983.

Kojève, Alexander. *Introduction to the Reading of Hegel: Lectures on the Phenomenology of Spirit*. New York: Basic Books, 1969.

Krahl, H. J. "Zum Verhältnis von 'Kapital' und Hegelscher Wesenslogik." In Negt, 1970.

Kroker, Arthur. *The Postmodern Scene*. Montreal: New World Perspectives, 1986.

Lebowitz, Michael. "Is Analytical Marxism Marxism?" *Science and Society* 52, no. 2 (1988).

Lenin, V. I. "Conspectus of Hegel's Book *The Science of Logic*." In *Collected Works*, vol. 38. London: Lawrence & Wishart, 1976.

Levine, Andrew, E. Sober, and E. O. Wright. "Marxism and Methodological Individualism." *New Left Review* 162, (1987).

Löwith, Karl. *From Hegel to Nietzsche*. New York: Anchor Books, 1967.

Lukács, Georg. *The Young Hegel*. Cambridge, Mass., MIT Press, 1976.

Lyotard, Jean. *The Postmodern Condition: A Report on Knowledge*. Minneapolis: University of Minnesota Press, 1984.

MacGregor, David. *The Communist Ideal in Hegel and Marx*. Toronto: University of Toronto Press, 1984.

MacIntyre, A. C., ed. *Hegel: A Collection of Critical Essays*. New York: Doubleday Books, 1972.

Mandel, Ernest. *Marxist Economic Theory*. New York: Monthly Reveiw Press, 1971.

______. *Late Capitalism*. London: Verso Press. 1975.

______. and A. Freeman. *Ricardo, Marx, Sraffa*. London: Verso Press, 1984.

Marx, Karl. *Theories of Surplus Value*, vol. 2. Moscow: Progress Publishers, 1968.

______. *Theories of Surplus Value*, vol. 3. Moscow: Progress Publishers, 1971.

______. *Grundrisse*. New York: Vintage Press, 1973.

______. *Capital*, 3 volumes. Moscow: Progress Publishers, 1978.

______. *Selections*, ed. A Wood, New York: Macmillan, 1988.

______ and Fredrick Engels. *Collected Works*, vols. 3 and 5. New York: International Publishers, 1976.

______. *Selected Writings*, ed. D. McLellan. Oxford: Oxford University Press, 1977.

______. *The Marx-Engels Reader*, ed. R. Tucker. New York: Norton Press, 1979.

______. *Letters on "Capital"*. London: New Park, 1983.

McCarney, Joseph. *The Real World of Ideology*. Atlantic Highlands, N.J.: Humanities Press, 1980.

______. "A New Marxist Paradigm?" *Radical Philosophy* 43, (1986).

______. *Marxism and the Crisis of Social Theory*. London: Verso Press, 1990.

Meek, Ronald. *Economics and Ideology and Other Essays*. London: Chapman & Hall, 1967.

Mepham, John. "From the *Grundrisse* to *Capital*: The Making of Marx's Method." In Mepham and Ruben, 1979.

______ and David Ruben, eds. *Issues in Marxist Philosophy*, vol. 1. Atlantic Highlands, N.J.: Humanities Press, 1979.

Morishima, Michio. *Marx's Economics*. Cambridge: Cambridge University Press, 1973.

Murray, Patrick, and J. Schuler. "Postmodernism in a French Context." *History of European Ideas*, no. 9 (1988).

Negt, Oskar, ed. *Aktualität und Folgen der Philosophie Hegels*. Frankfurt: Suhrkamp, 1970.

Nielsen, Kai. *Marxism and the Moral Point of View*. Boulder, Col.: Westview Press, 1988.

Norman, Richard, and S. Sayers. *Hegel, Marx and Dialectic*. Atlantic Highlands, N.J.: Humanities Press, 1980.

Oeing-Hanhoff, Ludger. "Hegels Trinitätslehre. Zur Aufgabe ihrer Kritik und Rezeption." *Theologie und Philosophie* 52 (1975).

Ollman, Bertell. *Alienation*. Cambridge: Cambridge University Press, 1976.

Pelczynski, Z. A. *Hegels Political Philosophy: Problems and Perspectives*. New York: Cambridge University Press, 1971.

______. *State and Civil Society: Studies in Hegel's Political Philosophy*. New York: Cambridge University Press, 1984.

Pinkard, Terry. "The Logic of Hegel's Logic." In Inwood, 1985.

______. *Hegel's Dialectic: The Explanation of Possibility*. Philadelphia: Temple University Press, 1988.

Popper, Karl. "What Is Dialectic?" *Mind* 49 (1940).

______. *The Open Society and Its Enemies*. Princeton, N.J.: Princeton University Press, 1966.

Poster, Mark. "Semiology and Critical Theory: From Marx to Baudrillard." In Spanos, Bove, and O'Hara, 1982.

Reichelt, Hans. *Zur logischen Struktur des Kapitalbegriffs*. Frankfurt: Europaische Verlagsanstalt, 1973.

Roemer, John. *A General Theory of Exploitation and Class*. Cambridge, Mass.: Harvard University Press, 1982.

______. "Property Relations vs. Surplus Value in Marxian Exploitation." *Philosophy and Public Affairs* 11, no. 4 (1982).

______. "New Directions in the Theory of Exploitation and Class." *Politics and Society* 11, no. 3 (1982).

______. "Unequal Exchange. Labor Migration and International Capital Flows: A Theoretical Synthesis." In Desai, 1983.

______. "Exploitation, Class, and Property Relations." In Ball and Farr, 1984.

______, ed. *Analytical Marxism*. Cambridge: Cambridge University Press, 1986.

______. "Should Marxists Be Interested in Exploitation?" In Roemer, *Analytical Marxism*. 1986.

______. "'Rational Choice' Marxism: Some Issues of Method and Substance." In Roemer, *Analytical Marxism*, 1986.

Rosdolsky, Roman. *The Making of Marx's "Capital"*. London: Pluto Press, 1977.

Rubin, I. I. *Essays on Marx's Theory of Value*. Montreal: Black Rose Books, 1982.

Schlitt, Dale. *Hegel's Trinitarian Claim*. Leiden: E. J. Brill, 1984.

Schmidt, Alfred, ed. *Beiträge zur Marxistischen Erkenntnis Theorie*. Frankfurt: Suhrkamp, 1969.

Shaikh, Anwar. "The Transformation from Marx to Sraffa." In Mandel and Freeman, 1984.

Smith, Tony. *The Logic of Marx's "Capital."* Albany: SUNY Press, 1990.

______. *The Role of Ethics in Social Theory: Essays from A Habermasian Perspective*. Albany: SUNY Press, 1991.

Spanos, William, P. Bove, and D. O'Hara. *The Question of Textuality*. Bloomington: Indiana University Press, 1982.

Splett, Joerg. *Die Trinitätslehre G. W. F. Hegels*. Munich: Alber, 1965.

Steedman, Ian. *Marx After Sraffa*. London: New Left Books, 1977.

Suchting, W. A. *Marx and Philosophy*. London: Macmillan, 1986.

Theunissen, Michael. *Hegels Lehre vom absoluten Geist als theologischer-politischer Traktat*. Berlin: de Gruyter, 1970.

Trotsky, Leon. *The Death Agony of Capitalism*. New York: Pathfinder Press, 1973.

Weber, Max. *Economy and Society*. 2 volumes. New York: Bedminister Press, 1968.

White, Alan. *Absolute Knowledge: Hegel and the Problem of Metaphysics*. Athens: Ohio University Press, 1983.

Winfield, Richard Dien. *The Just Economy*. New York: Routledge, Chapman & Hall, 1988.

Wood, Alan. *Karl Marx*. Lodon: Routledge & Kegan Paul. 1982.

Zelený, Jindřich. *Die Wissenschaftslogik bei Marx und 'Das Kapital.'* Frankfurt: Europaische Verlagsanstalt, 1962.

Index